Prisoners Victory Parade

Extraordinary Stories of Maximum Saints & Former Prisoners

Yong Hui V. McDonald

"I was privileged to help edit *Prisoners Victory Parade*. As I read the stories I rejoiced and cried with each of the authors. I was inspired to look at my own plans for my Lord — are they big enough? I'll be done with my own sentence in less than eight months, and I hope to be one of those who has another victory story. The battle is not ours — it's God's. These stories have imparted to me that He loves us so much that He has graciously shared these victories with us. I know all who read this book will be blessed as well, and I will prayerfully hope they too will experience a victory from God."
—Justine Lenzini, editor, writer, an inmate at ACDF

"Being a part of Transformation Project Prison Ministry (TPPM) wasn't my plan at all, but God's. My involvement helped me to understand the depths of other people's pain and suffering. I am excited to be a part of TPPM, knowing that my work will affect others in a positive way; it will help others spiritually. *Maximum Saints* stories have a greatly anointing touch and are encouraging. Reading them helped me to understand God's love and helped me to learn to love Him and love others as well. I thought, 'I am helping the chaplain to help others.' While I was helping her, I was the one who was blessed the most. Wow! I was planting seeds without even realizing it. I personally believe that God's power has no limits. This is the reason I will not be surprised to see TPPM reaching out across the nation and even around the world."
—Mireya Vizcarra, editor, writer, an inmate at ACDF

"Once you have read about the real life stories of ACDF inmates, you will have an understanding of their pain and battle to overcome the devil's temptations. The victories that the inmates have endured is emotionally and spiritually heart warming. We have an amazing opportunity to change our lives through the grace of God. The decision we make to follow Christ is more important than anything we will ever do, it's a matter of life or death."
—Robert Garcia, editor, writer, an inmate at ACDF

PRISONERS VICTORY PARADE
Extraordinary Stories of Maximum Saints & Former Prisoners

Copyright ©2011 by Yong Hui V. McDonald also known as Vescinda McDonald. All rights reserved.

Books, audio books, DVDs written and produced by Yong Hui V. McDonald are also available. To purchase, contact www.griefpathway.com or email at griefpwv@gmail.com or order by phone: 1-800-booklog, 1-800-266-5564. GriefPathway Ventures, LLC, P.O. Box 220, Brighton, CO 80601. Adora Productions is an imprint of the GriefPathway Ventures, LLC.

Except for brief excerpts for review purposes, no part of this publication may be reproduced, stored in a retrieval system, or transmitted in any form or by any means – electronic, mechanical, photocopying, recording, or otherwise without the prior permission of the copyright owners. All rights reserved.

All Scripture quotations are taken from The Holy Bible, New International Version. Copyright © 1973, 1978, 1984 International Bible Society. All rights reserved.
Published by Adora Productions
Printed in the United States of America
ISBN: 978-1-935791-37-9
Cover Designed by Lynette McClain
McClain Productions, www.mcclainproductions
Cover Art & Design Copyright ©2011 Adora Productions
Photographs for cover: Mike Goins
First Printing: September 2011

1. Prisoners 2. Prison Memoirs 3. Spiritual Growth

CONTENTS

DEDICATION
Drawing (1) "Dedication" by Burnie
ACKNOWLEDGMENTS

Chapter 1: Leading Hands...........8
Chapter 2: Prisoners Victory Parade
Drawing (2) "Maximum Saints" by Burnie.........17
1. "A MISSON TRIP" — Jonathan Willis.........18
2. "THE POWER OF PRAYER" — Cortez Henderson.....22
3. "A GREAT PREACHER" — Charles Frederick and Waymonn Boston........24
4. "A MAN IN A NEW MEXICO PRISON" — Theodore Sanchez and David Waltley........27
5. "BANGING ON THE WALL"........29
6. "STOPPED A FIGHT"........30
7. "A GRIEVING WOMAN".........32
8. "CHRISTMAS IN JAIL" — Carlos Tanguma and Michael O'Connor........33
9. "A JAIL CHAPLAIN" — Richard Smittal........36
10. "FINDING HOPE" — Jason Vigil and Michah Collins........39
11. "GOD CAN FORGIVE ANYONE" — Samuel Uribe........42
12. "ANOINTED TOUCH" — Mireya Vizcarra......... ..45
13. "GOD IS REAL" — Lakiesha Vigil........50
14. "NO LONGER SERVE SATAN" — Timothy Garcia........53
15. "ALL THINGS ARE POSSIBLE" — Heather Lopez........54
16. "A HAPPY RABBIT" — Crystal Gillespie........56
17. "DANCING FOR THE LORD" — Donna Tabor........58
18. "HE WAS SAD TO LEAVE JAIL" — Greg Lisco.......61
19. "A CHAPLAIN'S TRUSTEE" — Peter Nguyen........63

20. "A MAN WAS SAVED" — John King........64
21. "WHY I AM SO HAPPY" — Jose Marquez and Omar Castaneda........66
22. "I THANK JESUS" — Monica Valdez...............70
23. "A LIFE SAVED" — Justine Lenzini.............. 74
24. "THE ARTIST" — Charles Polk and his drawing (3) "Jesus on the Cross"........78

Chapter 3: Extraordinary Stories of Former Prisoners
1. "NEW HOPE MINISTRIES" — Founder, Rev. Ray Chavez........79
2. "ABC MINISTRIES" — Founder, George Medley....85
3. "NO REGRETS" — Irene Chavez, The Organizer of ABC Ministries, wife of George Medley........93
4. "OPEN DOOR, YOUTH GANG ALTERNATIVES" — Founder, Rev. Leon Kelly........103

Chapter 4: Reflections by Yong Hui McDonald
1. The Man's Tears........112
2. Why Lord?........112
3. God Was There........113
4. Crystal........114
5. Transformation........115
6. Make No Little Plans........117
7. Revival........122
8. One Million Dream Project........125
9. Unexpected Call........126

Chapter 5: How to Start Prisoners' Book Project........129
Chapter 6: A Prayer of Blessing........132
Chapter 7: Invitations
1. An Invitation to Accept Christ........132
2. An Invitation to Transformation Project Prison Ministry (TPPM) & "One Million Dream Project"........133
3. How to purchase *Maximum Saints* books

About the Author..........135

DEDICATION

I dedicate this book to my loving heavenly Father, my Lord Jesus, and to the Holy Spirit. Also to all the prisoners and their families all over the world.

Drawing "Dedication"
By
Burnie

ACKNOWLEDGMENTS

I thank God for my wonderful mother, for her love and prayers for me. I believe that because of her prayers the Lord has blessed me and my ministry beyond my imagination. She has been my cheerleader, spiritual mentor and a wonderful mother who treated all her children with love and respect. She planted the seeds of faith in my heart from early childhood.

I am deeply indebted to my wonderful husband Keith, who died in a car accident in July 2008, and is with the Lord. Keith brought healing in my heart and helped my ministry preparation more than anyone I've ever met. I thank the Lord for giving me such a wonderful friend and husband for 30 years. I also thank my beautiful children, Fletcher and Nicole. I pray that God will bless them beyond their imagination in all areas of life.

I am grateful for all Adams County Detention Facility saints who helped me edit this book: Kathleen W. Cooper, Brittany Espinosa, Rita Finney, Robert Garcia, Felonis Hernandez, Cheryl Killion, Justine Lenzini, Russett Loucks, Heather Lopez, Joseph Corey Luman, Lisa Newberry, Jennifer Spade, Juanita Tamayo, Laquesha Thomas, Lakiesha Vigil, Mireya Vizcarra, and Mary Voogt. I thank Burnie and Charles Polk for the drawings. Also, I thank Amy Penn for helping me edit this book. God bless you all!

Finally, I give glory to Jesus. Without Him, this book could not have been written.

Chapter 1

Leading Hands

<u>1. How Did *Maximum Saints* Book Start?</u>
I started working as a chaplain at Adams County Detention Facility (ACDF) in Brighton, Colorado in 2003. After I started working as a chaplain, there was one thing that bothered me. Many inmates requested spiritually nurturing books, but the chaplain's office didn't have enough books. We relied on the donation of books.

I started Transformation Project Prison Ministry (TPPM) in 2005 with the help of many friends to bring more books to help ACDF inmates. TPPM started producing *Maximum Saints* books which contain inmates powerful stories of transformation. First I thought about making only one inmates' book, but after I saw the impact of their stories, we started producing more books.

TPPM has grown, we have produced books in English and Spanish and DVDs. They are distributed through chaplains in jails, prisons and homeless shelters at no charge, nationwide.

As of 2011, TPPM has produced eight English books, two Spanish books and four DVDs. We are continuously producing books and DVDs. If someone would have told me that TPPM would be distributing more than 100,000 copies of books and DVDs within seven years, I wouldn't have believed it, but it happened. Every time I work on a *Maximum Saints* book, I am so blessed. God is leading this project and I feel so privileged to be a part of it. The letters we receive from many different jails and prisons across the nation shows that there is a need for these kind of books.

2. The Assignment

On May 13, 2011, God asked me to write a book to help the families of the incarcerated. He told me to put together Maximum Saints stories in this book from a chaplain's point of view.

I couldn't quite understand why I should do it at first. I thought families needed something else. Why not write a book on how to visit prisoners. Maybe details of what they want to know from a chaplain when a family member is incarcerated. I started a book like that about five years ago, but I quit writing because I didn't feel God was leading it.

This time it was clear to me that God didn't want me to write other information, but write about Maximum Saints stories for the families of the prisoners. Actually, I didn't want to write this book at first because I was already working on another *Maximum Saints* book.

3. The Stories of Horror

For the next two days, I wondered what families of the incarcerated would want to hear from a chaplain. While thinking about this, I read two books.

The first book was called, *Eyes of the Tailless Animals, Reflections of a North Korean Woman*, written by Soon Ok Lee, a woman who survived harsh labor conditions in North Korea. While I was reading the book, I was horrified by the conditions and treatments of prisoners in North Korea. As the title indicated, prisoners were treated worse than animals. They suffered from hard, long labors. People's lives didn't seem to have any value. Some people were so hungry they ate dirt, because it seemed to taste good, and they ultimately died.

Also, Christians were persecuted and tortured. Some people died after acid was poured on them. Many died just because of their faith. I was shaken by the stories. There was no room for discussion of human rights, human dignity or need for religious freedom.

Another book I read was called *There Is No One that God Cannot Heal*, by Hyo Jin Park who used to be the prison captain in South Korea. This man had a reputation of being a man from "hell," and he was proud of it. He treated prisoners harshly. Some prisoners even plotted to kill him.

After this captain became a Christian, he realized what he was doing was wrong. He grieved for the way he treated the prisoners.

One day this captain was so remorseful he asked for forgiveness from a prisoner, whom he had previously beat with a bat until the man was unconscious. This prisoner didn't respond. Then God told the captain to get on his knees and ask for forgiveness. He was embarrassed, so he looked to see if there was anyone around.

When he didn't see anyone, he got on his knees and begged for forgiveness. The prisoner was touched by the captain's change of attitude and behavior, and became a Christian. This captain helped many death row prisoners to find God as well. He prayed before their executions. Then after the execution, he and a group of Christian volunteers took care of the prisoners' bodies.

Mr. Park described how he was helping death row inmates and how he was touched by them before they were prosecuted. I was deeply touched as well by how death row inmates can smile, sing hymns, praise God and proclaim their faith to the executioners before they were executed. A couple years ago, I read a Korean Newspaper saying that South Korea abolished the death penalty. The books I read gave me more understanding of the suffering of prisoners.

Even though there is religious freedom in South Korea, prisoners' rights are not protected from the abuse and violence from prison guards. Humiliation and suffering is accepted as punishment for breaking the law and just because these people are prisoners. It's a real sad situation when people justify violence and cause pain when dealing with prisoners.

4. American Prisoners' Rights

After I read these two books, I felt I didn't have anything to write. American law protects the rights of prisoners, that their basic needs are met: food, shelter, safety and religious freedom. Prisoners sue jails and prisons if their rights are violated. Facilities have to pay the consequences if they didn't obey the law.

In our facility, inmates have three hot meals every day, have air-conditioning in the summer, heating in the winter, receive medical treatment (surgeries and medicines) for free. They can see doctors for a small fee, but if they don't have any money, they don't have to pay.

Many programs are offered to inmates such as: life-skills, anger management, alcohol and drug recovery classes, English as a Second Language (ESL) and GED classes for free. There are mental health services, social workers, a psychiatrist, nurses and on-call doctors that are always available for inmates in the medical unit.

Our facility has two full-time chaplains who provide spiritual support and religious counseling. We provide grief and crisis counseling when there is a suicide, or a critical incident. Also, chaplains deliver death notifications to inmates and support inmates in times of difficulties.

We have many volunteers leading worship services and Bible studies every week, including a celebrate recovery class which helps people who struggle with addiction.

Inmates can sign up to attend any of these classes. However, people in the medical unit, isolation unit, protective custody, maximum unit or disciplinary unit have restrictions on participating in most of the programs; however, when they go back to general population, they can sign up.

Not like state prisons, where people are assigned to work and get paid very little, ACDF inmates are mostly waiting for trials, sentencing or serving short sentences. So, inmates can watch TV, play cards, play basketball in the yard and read books; although books are limited. Families can send the books through book stores if the books are appropriate. If their family or others put money on an inmate's account, he/she can buy phone time to make outside phone calls and can purchase snacks, stamps, notebooks, ramen noodles, coffee, etc. from the commissary.

Those who don't have any money will receive a limited number of stamps, envelopes and paper so they can write to their family. Inmates don't have to do laundry except those who are working in the laundry as trustees who will get less time in jail. Inmates don't have to cook, unless they are kitchen workers who will get less time in jail.

When I think about homeless people who do not have a place to sleep and lack food and medical attention, prisoners have more privileges than homeless people. I was surprised to find out that some people in fact put themselves in jail to avoid a harsh winter. That's a reality for some people and that's the true, honest confession of some of the inmates.

Even though American jails seem to be better in terms of human rights and meeting the basic needs, jail is a sad, painful, horrible place for most people. Many are separated from their families and devastated. Many are losing everything: job, house, car, self-respect, even family. Many are traumatized by the fact that they are incarcerated.

In fact, some people can get hurt by others, especially if they are associated with gangs. There are high suicide rates in jails and prisons. Fights break out. For many reasons there are many hurting inmates. Gang violence and sexual abuse in jails and prisons do exist. These incident are a very small part of prison life, although it depends on which jail or prison you may be incarcerated in. Security and safety is a big part of what facility officers are working hard to achieve.

Unfortunately, the media amplifies crimes and violence in jails and prisons, which affects the perception of prisoners. Even those who have committed horrible crimes are actually hurting and are in need of healing. America has the highest prison population of 2.3 million. America also has the highest penalty for crimes because I don't believe American people are any worse than people in other countries.

5. Perception

I was thinking about what I should focus on writing to help families of prisoners, so I asked my trustee who helps when I hold worship services, "What do you think families of the incarcerated would like to know about prisoners?"

He replied, "I think they need to know that we are safe. The TV and media portray prison as a terrible place. Actually, it's safe inside. They have no idea how we are doing inside."

I thought that was a very interesting point. One day an inmate's father passed away. His mother came to deliver the message to her son. I knew this inmate because he attended church and I have talked with him before. His mother said, "I worry about his safety every moment while he is in jail. I cannot let go of this worry."

"Why?" I asked. "He is smiling, carrying the Bible and reading it. This is actually a safe place for him. He told me he was growing spiritually and shared how God was blessing him. Why do you worry? He comes to chaplain's worship services and I know he is doing fine. You need to give God your worry and take care of yourself."

Jails and prisons can be a safe place for those who are involved in alcohol, drugs, gangs or even homeless people. If they are outside with the wrong people at the wrong time, they can hurt themselves and others or even be killed.

Many people asked me, "How can you work in a jail? Do you feel safe?" I replied, "Jail is safer than walking on the street." Many people perceive prisoners as dangerous people. What they don't see is that everyone has goodness in them. They are people just like anyone else. Many prisoners I have met are very kind, compassionate, and considerate. That's what outside people do not realize. Yes, there are few who may be dangerous but those type of people are outside as well.

6. What Is Missing?

I was attending a retreat and a pastor asked me if there is any hope for prisoners to change. Without hesitation, I said, "Yes. There are many people who are trying to make changes but many of their stories have not come out. Many prisoners are serving God and helping others. They make a difference. Also, there are many former prisoners who are making a difference in the community."

This pastor with his eyes wide open said, "Really, I haven't seen anyone who is changed, so I have a difficult time believing it." I see how the public has a preconceived notion and it is affected by the media portrayal of prisoners. I have seen it through the eyes of a pastor.

When people see prisons and prisoners only through media, something is really missing. I had no idea that there were so many saints in jails and prisons before I started working as a chaplain. I don't watch much TV but I was still affected by the media through the newspapers.

I finally realized why God asked me to bring attention to Maximum Saints stories for families of the prisoners. The Lord wanted me to bring out something that the media does not focus on or even recognize. That is the powerful inmate leaders' stories which gives us hope and encouragement. Can't the outside public understand that there are prisoners who are saving others from hurting themselves and others, even from suicide. I hear these kind of stories from inmates more than anyone because I am a chaplain.

After I started gathering stories, my original plan was to have only ACDF inmates' stories. When I thought I had finished the book, the Lord asked me to include the stories of former inmates who are making a difference in the community.

I couldn't understand why, I even resisted at first because I was so focused on prisoners' stories. Later I understood why. Their stories would not only give hope to the prisoners, but also their families. It would let the world know that there is hope for everyone who tries to follow God's lead in their lives. I finally said, "I get it Lord. I praise you for leading this book. You always have better ideas than mine."

7. Victory Parade

On June 25, 2010, God gave me the vision that Jesus was up front dancing and leading the prisoners who are serving Him. Jesus himself was a prisoner even though he didn't do anything wrong. He too was humiliated, tortured, suffered, crucified and died. Yet, Jesus is alive and brings hope. He understands what prisoners go through and he blesses them.

This spiritual vision gave me a glimpse of what I may see in heaven someday. Many of the saints I have ministered to in jails and prisons will be joining this procession with great joy, praising Jesus with others. There will be a reward for many prisoners who serve the Lord. But we don't have to wait to hear the stories of prisoners in heaven. I believe—with the help of the Holy Spirit—we can hear their stories right now. *Maximum Saints* books are doing just that. In reality, many incarcerated saints are already following the procession.

This book is only a little glimpse of how Jesus is leading and blessing many prisoners. I feel privileged to see this happening at ACDF. Have you heard any awesome stories that have blown you away? I have. I have heard so many stories that it has changed my perception of prisoners and how God is blessing these people.

Their testimonies are changing many others through the *Maximum Saints* books and DVDs. I cannot help but to cheer for what Jesus is doing through these prisoners and also former prisoners' testimonies. Praise God! I have found treasures on earth—saints at ACDF and their testimonies blessed me. *"They overcame him by the blood of the Lamb and by the word of their testimony; they did not love their lives so much as to shrink from death." (Revelation 12:11)*

Chapter 2

Prisoners Victory Parade

Maximum Saints are not necessarily classified as maximum inmates. I call them maximum saints because they use their gifts to the maximum.

Drawing "Maximum Saints"
By
Burnie

I have encountered many amazing ACDF inmate leaders and many of their stories have been published in different *Maximum Saints* books. Some will be published in the next book, *Maximum Saints All Things Are Possible*. I will share some of the ACDF saints stories and testimonies that made a difference in many others' lives and also in my spiritual journey.

1. "A MISSON TRIP" — Jonathan Willis

Jonathan was 25 years old when I met him. I have thanked God for Jonathan many times. It was a privilege and honor to meet him, even though his time here at ACDF was brief.

When I first met Jonathan, he was in a maximum security pod in A Module. I asked for someone to lead the song in one of the chaplain's worship services. Everyone pointed at Jonathan. Jonathan, a song writer and singer, shared his testimony and sermons in chaplain's worship services.

One day, Jonathan wanted to speak with a chaplain because he was concerned about his case. He shared that he had a difficult time focusing on serving the Lord at the time. A couple months later, this had changed since he moved to B Module. I saw the transformation in him. He looked happier after he started leading the Bible study and the prayer circle in his pod. He was very effective and his influence was powerful.

When the Transformation Project Prison Ministry (TPPM) was ready to make the second Maximum Saints DVD, I asked Jonathan to be a part of this project with his song and testimony. I was amazed by his enthusiasm and his talents, and I felt blessed by his contribution. He said he kept writing songs without knowing how God could use them.

Then one day Jonathan wanted to see me. I knew his

trial was coming up. Before he shared his struggles, I told him he did not have to tell me anything, but that he should obey what God was telling him to do to find peace. He agreed. He knew what God wanted him to do was tell the truth. He knew telling the truth would be costly and he may not ever be freed, but he followed what God told him to do. He pled guilty and was sentenced to life without parole.

After his sentencing, I went to visit him. I expected that he would come out with a stressed, gloomy, sad, and depressed look on his face. I was wrong. Jonathan had a big smile and shared how he felt good about telling the truth, because that's what God wanted him to do. He shared that he was ready to serve the Lord for the rest of his life in prison. He also said, "Chaplain, I received a letter from Adam's mom, and it encouraged me so much. All I am going through is worth it when I think about the letter. I will do anything to receive letters like that." Adam was an inmate in Jonathan's pod.

The next time I visited, Jonathan sang a song for me and my assistant. I was so touched that it almost made me cry. We went there to comfort and encourage Jonathan. Instead, he was ministering to us. I knew there was hope. He knew how to turn misery into joy by finding purpose in his life. He found joy in an impossible situation by making a commitment to serve the Lord for the rest of his life.

As we were talking, Jonathan said somehow he remembered what he used to pray. His prayer was to be a missionary, and he said he will be a missionary for the Lord in prison. A couple of days later, I remembered Jonathan's comment about Adam's mom's letter. I asked if he could share it with me. He told me he had already mailed the letter to his Mom the night before. While I was talking with him, a mail lady was picking up the mail. Jonathan ran to her and got the letter and shared it with me. Here is part of the letter from Adam's mom:

> Dear Jonathan,
> Hi, I am Adam's mom. I wanted to write to you to tell you, "Thank you so much for being the messenger I prayed for." I had asked our Heavenly Father to send Adam a messenger in jail to speak His word to him, and in my heart I believe you are that messenger.
> I have never heard my son so humble, and speaking of our Lord so gracefully. You have been a blessing to him. He tells me how much he sees the Holy Spirit within you. Please continue to use what our Heavenly Father has given you, which is a soft spirit to preach His word to the lost.
> Jesus is coming for His church very, very soon. You remind me of Paul in the Bible. He wrote most of the New Testament. Be strong and listen to His voice, for you are on the path to win souls for the kingdom, and your rewards will be great in heaven. I'm praying for you.
> I would like to continue to write to you and send some sermons your way from our pastor. Please write back and give me the address of where they are sending you. Be strong and know that there are brothers and sisters in Christ praying with you and for you. God bless you. Adam's mom

I reread the letter and thanked God for Jonathan. Before Jonathan left our facility, he shared with me that in prison there is a job program in which he could make some money. When he does that, he sends the money to support the TPPM. I couldn't believe it. He is the one who needs it more, but he was thinking about others.

Though Jonathan has left ACDF, his legacy lives on.

One day I was leading worship in A Module, and I asked inmates to share their stories of transformation and what the turning points were for them. One inmate shared how he met Jonathan Willis in B Module. He mentioned how Jonathan, who had received a life sentence, was calm, peaceful, and witnessed to others. This encouraged him. He shared that he accepted Christ and decided to change his gang life because of him. This man also added that he was baptized by me one day in B Module because Jonathan had shared Christ with him. Then I remembered the day when Jonathan was sitting next to this man, telling me how this man accepted the Lord and wanted to be baptized. Before Jonathan left, he gave him a study Bible that he had received from his mother. This man opened the Bible showing where Jonathan's name was.

One day I got a phone call from a reporter at the Denver Post newspaper who wanted to know more about the TPPM. He explained that he was writing an article about jail conversion and how real it is. I told him it is real. Many incarcerated people are hurting, but God is blessing many who are open to Him. He asked me what makes me believe that Christianity has the answer to transformation. I told him that Christian belief offers a spiritual map, good morals, direction towards a loving God and loving others, and has the path for transformation through Jesus Christ. I have seen many transformed lives through Christianity that I have not seen through any other religion.

The reporter told me he was interviewing people by visiting different facilities and ministry settings. The reporter came to our facility and interviewed some inmates and also went to interview Jonathan who had already moved to another facility. God reminded me that He is honored when people share their stories of transformation in Christ. This story was published in *Maximum Saints Dream*, and is titled "A Discovery of Maximum Saints." and his story "Fear

Within Us" was published in the book, *Maximum Saints Make No Little Plans*.

2. "THE POWER OF PRAYER" — Lloyd Henderson

One day, when I was gathering inmates for chaplain's worship from F Module, there were some verbal altercations between two people on the second floor. The control tower deputy called for assistance, and in the mean time, I saw something I had never seen before.

All of the men formed a big circle holding hands and prayed the Lord's prayer. About midway through the prayer, the deputy from F2300 came in. When the prayer was over, everyone was calm, and ready to go to worship. I told the deputy that if I had any problems at the service, I would call him. The service went fine.

The next day, I visited the man who was shouting at the other man on the day of service. I told him how upset I was by his actions, how violent words or actions wouldn't bring any good results, but would cause a destructive ripple effect for many people. After I explained my views on how to resolve the conflict, he agreed with what I had said, and told me that he would do better next time, by trying his hardest so this wouldn't happen again.

I also visited F2200 to thank the two leaders who suggested to the others to hold hands and pray. I asked the leaders to prepare a sermon on how to resolve conflicts peacefully. The following week, the man who had done the shouting apologized to the other man, and to the whole group. Then, Lloyd Henderson, one of the leaders from F2200 preached about how God helped them to have a peaceful resolution and avoid conflict through prayer.

Mr. Henderson was a powerful preacher and he preached in chaplain's worship many times. Here is what he preached:

"THE POWER OF PRAYER" by Lloyd Henderson

On July 1, 2006, the Chaplain and a guest speaker entered pod 2200. She called out the afternoon worship. We all started to gather around to fulfill God's purpose. While we were moving forward to exit the doors, and walking down the hallway (before we came close to the elevators), we could hear and see two guys having an altercation. The devil was really playing his part. This is something that we had never experienced before at worship time. As the two men were using vulgar and abusive language, their anger began to rise — like water in a boiling pot. I paused, and I questioned myself, "Where is the love, peace, and kindness in their hearts?" They continued to savagely attack one another with words.

What a great way of showing maturity. They still had not realized that their fight was not about them. It was about the Lord, and while they continued, as we were waiting for the elevator, the power of the Lord moved us into a prayer circle. We began saying the Lord's Prayer from *Matthew 6:9-13*. Still, we knew the devil was right there in the midst of it all, trying to tempt us, and destroy our spirit. We will never let the devil win, as sure as my heart, my mind, and my gut were speaking. We all continued to go on to fellowship, even though this situation had occurred.

This was an example for us all. *"When I was a child, I talked like a child, I thought like a child, and I reasoned like a child. When I became a man, I put childish ways behind me."* (1 Corinthians 13:11) It could have turned out worse than it did, because in this day and age, violence has begotten violence.

Stop and think. Life is too short! Think before you react to others (and your surroundings), so that you don't have to regret any foolish actions or destructive behavior. Now you have to prove only one thing: the good inside your heart, for that is what the Lord Jesus Christ sees within you.

You all have received the gifts of faith, hope, and love which come from God's armor.

This was published in the book *Maximum Saints Make No Little Plans.*

3. "A GREAT PREACHER" — Charles Frederick

In Chaplain's Worship services, I try to encourage inmates to share their testimonies and preach because God asked me to train the leaders from the beginning of my ministry.

When I announced that I wanted people who have a gift of teaching and preaching to lead in Chaplain's worship service, Charles Frederick volunteered. He preached many times. I was amazed by his sermons and great presentations. He was one of the best preachers I have ever heard both outside and inside jail. I even invited one of my missionary friends to come and listen to his sermon. She also marveled at his sermon and encouraged him to use his gifts to serve the Lord.

Once Mr. Frederick shared that when he went to prison previously he was talking without thinking, using many cuss words. Then that night when he was in his cell, the Lord told Mr. Frederick to share Christ with his new cell mate. He resisted thinking he had made a mistake, talked carelessly with others, and the man heard what he had said. But he didn't have peace and he knew God was asking him to share, so he told his cell mate about God. The man said, "I was praying that someone would share God with me." With that, Mr. Frederick learned how to obey the Holy Sprit's leading. God was using him no matter what. He had made mistakes, but his cell mate needed to hear the message of Christ and that encouraged him.

There was an interesting story about him. When Mr.

Fredrick was in a medium security unit, he was leading the Bible study and he was preparing to preach the following week. Just a couple of days before he preached, he was moved to the next room which was maximum security. Maximum inmates are not supposed to mix with the medium security people in worship services. Maximum security inmates are not allowed to mix with other maximum inmates in different pods even in worship. But I wanted him to preach, so I talked with the Captain and the Sergeant. They let Mr. Frederick preach to his old pod, the medium inmates. He was wearing orange and white strips, maximum security inmate clothes, while all the other inmates wore blue and white stripes which is medium security.

What's amazing is Mr. Frederick's leadership. Before he was housed in B Module Pod 3, no one was attending the chaplain's worship. Then as soon as he went in, he started a Bible study and many people started attending chaplain's worship service. I could see the positive impact that Mr. Frederick was making in that pod. His sermons and stories are published in different *Maximum Saints* books and have made a positive impact on many people.

After Mr. Frederick was sentenced, he was preaching and said that he wasn't worried about his time in prison. He said what was important was to serve the Lord. Shortly there after he moved on to state prison.

In 2011, a man named Waymonn Boston shared his encounter with Mr. Frederick. He wrote: "I was sent to prison in Walsenberg, Colorado, where they had a faith pod and I knew what I needed to do. I got into the program and with the help of other inmates, I began to find God. Then I met Charles Fredrick, who told his story in the first *Maximum Saints* book, *Maximum Saints Never Hide in the Dark*. With his love and guidance, I began to believe that there was still hope for me too. I got baptized and studied the Word day and night for almost a whole year."

Boston mentioned how he was mentored by Mr. Frederick when he was in prison. One day after one of the chaplain's worship services, a man asked me if the people who had a transformation would continue to keep up with their changed lives and serve the Lord when they move into the state prison.

My answer is yes. I have no doubt that these people will serve the Lord because they have found the joy of knowing and serving the Lord. Mr. Frederick was one of the examples. He was keeping up with his good works and I was hearing through others how much he had impacted them.

When people taste the joy of loving God, they cannot quit serving. They have finally found the purpose of living. Our life is for the Lord and serving God brings Him joy and also joy in our hearts. These people found the secret of fulfillment that many others never realize.

There is nothing like loving the Lord and putting Him first. There is nothing that can be compared to the joy of serving the Lord. Mr. Frederick knew this. His sermons kept coming out, even after he left because he wrote them and gave them to me.

When I work on the *Maximum Saints* books, God is reminding me to put in different people's sermons, and his is one of them. His sermons are going to many places to help many people.

Mr. Frederick's sermons are in different *Maximum Saints* books. The latest one is in *Maximum Saints Forgive,* the sermon called "The Man."

Mr. Boston also preached in chaplain's worship services many times. His sermons motivated and helped others to experience transformation. With one of the worship services he preached, I felt the Holy Spirit's power. His story will be coming out in the book, *Maximum Saints All Things*

Are Possible and *Maximum Saints* DVD as well.

4. "A MAN IN A NEW MEXICO PRISON" — Theodore Sanchez

Occasionally, God tells me who is called to the ministry and I need to encourage them to use their gifts. One day God spoke to me that Mr. Theodore Sanchez was called to the ministry and that I needed to encourage him to preach in worship. I was busy so I didn't have the chance to do that. Then one day I was walking toward B Module worship and God spoke to me again. I went to A Module where he was housed and told him God told me he was called to the ministry and he needed to prepare to preach. He said he would.

The first time he preached, he shared his experience in a New Mexico prison. It was an unbelievable story and I believe God wanted him to share it, and that's why He had me ask him to preach. While he was in one of the maximum security prisons, he was tormented by others who were gang members. He was not a gang member and they would bang on the walls so he couldn't sleep. In that hostile and isolated unit, a man ministered to him through the vent. This is what Mr. Sanchez wrote:

"A MAN IN A NEW MEXICO PRISON" by Theodore Sanchez

When I had ended up back in prison, I had made up my mind I was going to seek God's kingdom. I was known to be a Christian and talked to everyone. I hung out with mostly my race, the Hispanics (not to mention—that's what one's required to do when in prison). Anyhow, I was sent to Las Cruces, New Mexico, a prison only designed to house all of the notorious gang members known to run all of the prisons: a gang called (SNM) Syndicate of New Mexico.

I was locked down 24 hours a day and only left my cell escorted by two or more guards, handcuffed and shackled with a lead shank placed on the cuffs—just like walking a dog, only to be placed in another cage with a shower in it, to shower. All of the inmates tormented me, yelling catcalls all day and all night, literally taking turns, shifting on and off like soldiers do in the Army, pounding on the walls, not letting me sleep.

During this hell, about two months later, I was lying there on my bunk listening to all the madness, and there was a knock. It was coming from below me. I listened carefully because now I could hear someone with a really thick Spanish accent using Spanish slang. (I thought I was starting to finally lose my mind.)

I came to find out it was the person below me. He asked me my name, and then he introduced himself as David. He asked my permission if it was cool, that we start to talk to pass the time and to get to know each other. At first I was really cautious, because I thought he was trying to trick me to get information out of me; but I still went along. David advised me he was doing a life sentence for killing drug dealers execution-style. But, now he was a Christian man who had been locked up for 20 plus years and claimed he wasn't a gang member.

As time went on, we got to know each other quite a bit. Most of the time, David taught me the Bible. We played a game where we would read a chapter, and at the end of the chapter David would explain it to me so I could better understand it. He would also suggest that I memorize a key verse every day.

Every day he would pick a verse out of what we studied and turned it into a game, telling me that when he knocked, he wanted me to quote a certain verse. For example: *John 3:16: "For God so loved the world that He gave His only begotten Son, that whoever believes in Him should not perish but have everlasting life."*

David said not to cheat! And yes, sometimes I did, and, amazingly, David would know by how fast I answered the verse or how long it took, or just the way I worded it!

One day David called my name and said, "Theo (short for Theodore), soon you're going to be leaving Little Carnal (brother in Spanish), but I want to ask you something. Are you prejudiced?" I said, "No." He asked, "Are you sure? How do you feel about those miyas (Spanish slang for African American)?" I replied, "I'm cool with everybody. Why?" He said, "Just asking." I had thought to myself, "That's kind of weird," but I didn't think much of it. David woke me up one day screaming and hollering, "Theo, pack it up; you're leaving. But before you leave, I want to see you face-to-face, so I can give you a farewell gift."

I'm thinking to myself, "Yes, I can finally put a face to this voice I've been talking to him for almost a year through the vent." I hurried up packed and ran down the stairs to see the biggest, blackest man I had ever seen. I was talking to a black man the with a strong Spanish accent whole time. I was really surprised. We both had crocodile tears and started crying. He said, "My name is David Waltley." David gave me his Bible as a going-away gift. A Bible he had walked those deadly prison grounds with for 20 years or more. A Bible I didn't use very much, but still have to this day.

Mr. Sanchez's story was powerful. Who would have guessed that a man could minister to another man through a vent, but it happened. This story will be published in the book, *Maximum Saints All Things Are Possible*.

5. "BANGING ON THE WALL"

Whenever I have the spare time, I lead a prayer meeting inside the women's pods. If I have more time after the prayer, I counsel people individually or as a group. These are very productive times and I get to know who the leader is in different pods.

Many times when people had problems, their problems were solved through the prayer meetings. They were learning from each other; encouraged by others who were more mature. The inmate leaders are the ones who can help them. I am not always with them, but the inmates are in the same housing unit for 24 hours a day. Their ministry is very effective.

One day a deputy asked me to talk to a woman who started banging her head on the wall and crying in the pod as soon as she arrived in the module. I called her out and asked her how she was doing. This woman was in tremendous turmoil. She broke down in tears. She told me she was terrified because she was convinced that everyone in the pod was going to hurt her. However, I knew there were many maximum saints in that pod, but she didn't know it.

I told her I would be going into the pod to lead prayer and asked her to join. When I went inside and called for prayer, she came to the prayer circle. A couple of hours later, I called her out and asked her how she was doing. This time she came out with a big smile and said, "There are some nice people in there. They were fixing my hair." Instead of banging her head on the wall, this woman began focusing on growing in the Lord because some maximum saints in that pod encouraged her to do so.

This story was published in *Maximum Saints Make No Little Plan*s in the section, called "Discovery of the Maximum Saints."

6. "STOPPED A FIGHT"

One day I heard an amazing story from two deputies in one module. These deputies told me about a Vietnamese man who stopped a fight. Some inmates were just about to get into a fight and this man quickly got into the middle and separated them with such force that he stopped the fight before it even began. The deputies couldn't believe how fast this man was. This man's story is published in the book *Maximum Saints Make No Little Plans* in the section of "Discovery of the Maximum Saints."

There is more to the story about this man. This man had a difficult time speaking English but he faithfully attended chaplain's worship services. One day he asked me if he could have a Vietnamese Bible. But the Chaplain's office didn't have a Vietnamese Bible on hand.

I contacted different churches outside and I was told that they would mail me a Vietnamese Bible. I waited and waited. Time passed and they didn't send a Bible. A month passed, I still hadn't received it, so I called other churches. They didn't know where to get one either.

Shortly after I was going to attend a pastor's luncheon in Colorado Springs. While driving, God spoke to me that I needed to find a Vietnamese Bible that day. I immediately called one of my friends and asked her to go to a website to find a Christian Vietnamese book store address, so I could buy a Bible that day. After lunch was over, I still hadn't gotten a call back from my friend. Then a thought came to me. I thought Vietnamese restaurants should have the information. So, I called a restaurant and got an address for a book store.

When I arrived at my destination, all I saw was a big church but I didn't know where the book store was. Some people were working in the yard. I waved to them and said, "I am a chaplain at Adams County Detention Facility and one of the inmates requested a Vietnamese Bible. Is there anyone who has a Vietnamese Bible?"

They pointed to a man and said, "He is the pastor.

Ask him." The pastor told me to go inside the book store and I could pick one up there and I wouldn't have to pay for it.

When I went inside, two young women told me that they didn't have any Bibles and it would take a long time to get a Bible from Vietnam. I said I would pay for it if they could order one. They said it would take a long time and that they were sorry. I couldn't believe it. They weren't even willing to order a Bible for me. As I walked outside, I was so disappointed. I had to get a Bible that day.

I found the pastor and told him what they had said. He saw my disappointed look. I couldn't leave that place without a Bible. The pastor led me to his office and he gave me a little Bible that had only the New Testament.

I said, "This wouldn't do, I need a Bible with the Old and the New Testament." He asked me to wait and went into another room and brought me a brand new Bible. I asked, "What do I owe you?"

He said, "No, you don't have to pay. It's free. You can take it to him." I was so glad when I walked out of that place. The Bible had a price tag and it was more than $50. I thanked him. I told him he should come and visit the man and encourage him. He could donate some Vietnamese inspirational books to the chaplain's office and we could give it to him to read. I couldn't wait to give the Bible to the man. He looked so happy when he received the Bible. I asked him if he would like to have a visit from a Vietnamese pastor since I couldn't minister to him. He told me he would like that, so I made an arrangement with another Vietnamese pastor who was willing to visit this man. I was glad that this pastor had the heart to help a prisoner.

7. "A GRIEVING WOMAN"

One of the chaplain's duties is to deliver death notifications to inmates when their family members die or become seriously ill. One day I delivered a death notification to a woman. Her husband had died suddenly the night before. She was in shock. She was crying out loud in anguish and said, "I cannot believe it." She walked around the hallway and kept saying, "I cannot believe it."

I didn't have any words to say to this woman who was in shock and distressed. She said, "I would like to have a friend come out from my pod. I know she will understand me."

I called the woman out. When she learned her friend's husband had died, she was comforting her with the most soft and gentle voice. I could see why this woman wanted her friend to come out. In the midst of turmoil, she was comforted by the other inmate's presence and words. I was thankful that she had someone to help her in her distressful and heartbreaking situation.

8. "CHRISTMAS IN JAIL" — Carlos Tanguma and Michael O'Connor

In our facility, there is a candy and pop machine in minimum security. They also have the privilege of having a microwave. People can buy snacks and other necessities from the commissary, but someone has to put money on their account to get what they want. If a person does not have anyone to put money on their account, they cannot buy anything.

When an inmate left the facility, he sent ten dollars to ten other inmates who were housed in the module he had been in. It happened just before Christmas in 2004. Ten dollars isn't much to some, but to those who do not have anything, it is a lot. This man's generous gift brought so much joy to many inmates.

Another amazing Christmas story comes from a story which is written by Carlos Tanguma. His story is published in *Maximum Saints Make No Little Plans*.

"A CHRISTMAS STORY IN JAIL" by Carlos Tanguma

I've never seen so many indigent people in any of the six pods, but the "Maximum Saints" in F1300 just weren't willing to ignore their Christmas spirit which is the gift of Jesus Christ from God to everyone. They reminded me through their selfless actions that we are all capable of doing good.

These guys made sure everyone of us got a gift from the commissary list. I got a donut. It was an awesome donut because in this instance, it symbolized to me God's love, grace, and mercy which is in our hearts to show the world!

There was a healing glow on the faces of these selfless givers, along with Christmas cheer, as they passed out presents to the less fortunate. It was time for the Secret Santa gift unwrapping for which they had drawn names. One man, who sports a clean shaven head, unwrapped a comb and a shower cap! No, Christmas was not forgotten in F1300 this year. If we had a Christmas tree or a mantel from which to hang holiday stockings, their cheer would have been overshadowed by the smiles, laughter and brotherly love we experienced that morning.

Jesus said, "For I was hungry and you gave me something to eat, I was thirsty and you gave me something to drink, I was a stranger and you invited me in, I needed clothes and you clothed me, I was sick and you looked after me, I was in prison and you came to visit me....The King will reply, 'I tell you the truth, whatever you did for one of the least of these brothers of mine, you did for me." (Matthew 25:35-40)

Jesus is in you and in me. Let Him show you that everything is in His hands and that His hands are everywhere. This act of selfless giving was a miracle, friend. Miracles are a glimpse of what paradise is like: no sorrow, no pain, and no suffering. I received my money order about an hour after my Christmas donut, and in comparison, the donut shines brighter than gold.

Here is a story by Michael O'Connor who used to be a Chaplain's trustee and one of the editors of the first *Maximum Saints* book. His story was published in the book *Maximum Saints Never Hide in the Dark.*

"THE BEST PRESENT I GOT THIS YEAR" by Michael O'Connor

Friday, December 23, I returned to my pod after another day of inspiring worship as usual, all smiles and filled with the Holy Spirit. Sure enough a deputy was there handing out mail and I received two Christmas cards. As I started to climb the stairs to my cell, I saw the sad faces of a bunch of my fellow cellmates. I could almost read their minds, "O'C got another letter and I still haven't gotten a thing." My joy immediately went flat. I went in my cell and was visibly upset. I asked God to help me change the mood, it was almost Christmas. The next day after Christmas Eve services, I walked in my cell and saw the care packages we had all received. God told me what to do.

I took the Salvation Army pad of paper and drew 17 crosses on 17 sheets of paper. Underneath I wrote either scripture from the Bible or something like *"The most important part of Christmas is the first six letters, Merry Christmas, O'C."* Then I folded them up with a piece of the candy we were given and put the inmates' names on them. At 5:30am Christmas morning after they had eaten and went back to bed, I slipped them under their doors, feeling like Santa when my kids were young, my heart was smiling. I went back to bed.

I stayed in my cell reading until lunch time, almost

forgetting that it was Christmas. Then one at a time each individual came up to me throughout Christmas day to give me a heartfelt "Thank you." There was one young man about my son's age who came to me with tears in his eyes, shook my hand and said, "Thank you, Mr. O'C. It was the best present I got this year," as he turned and walked away. I ran to my cell and bawled my eyes out. Thanking God and wondered who benefited more from the little cards, them or me? Make the best of the time you have here and Jesus will walk with you the rest of the way out!

All these Christmas stories are gifts from those who care about others even in incarceration. I am truly blessed by their stories.

9. "A JAIL CHAPLAIN" — Richard Smittal

When I first met Richard, he was in maximum security. He was struggling with his court case. Slowly, I saw such a transformation in him that he shined among the inmates. He was a leader and I heard from many other inmates how he was helping them.

One day, Richard wanted to see me and told me that maximum inmates needed worship services. At the time, ACDF maximum inmates were only allowed to attend Anger Management classes. They could have individual religious counseling with the chaplains, but no worship services were offered to them.

I told him that the chaplains want to provide worship services for everyone but I was not able to convince the facility. Chaplains do not have the final decision on the matter. I asked him to write a letter to Mr. Sterritt Fuller, the program coordinator, to explain why maximum inmates needed worship. I told him I wanted to see his letter before he sent it. When Richard showed me the letter, I was very impressed. I told him he should send the letter to Mr. Fuller, write a kite (request form) to see him, and try to convince him why maximum inmates needed worship.

Richard convinced Mr. Fuller and I was delighted to see that Mr. Fuller was open to bringing the matter to the administration for approval. Mr. Fuller said, "You coached him well." I replied, "After you listen to so many maximum inmates that they need to attend worship services, you got to do something about it."

Richard asked me to ask other inmates to pray so maximum inmates can have worship services. Even though I prayed and asked others to pray so maximum inmates can have worship services, I was skeptical. Richard had more faith in this matter.

One day, while waiting for approval, he pointed at the contact room where worship services are held and said, "Chaplain, starting next month maximum inmates will be up there in the contact room and will be worshiping God. Please ask others to pray for this."

Finally, the facility approved the maximum inmates' worship services. I actually couldn't believe it. I thanked Richard's persistence. Many people rejoiced in the fact that maximum inmates could now attend worship services.

One day, while I was leading worship for A Module Pod 3 maximum inmates, the book *Maximum Saints Never Hide in the Dark* was published. I asked Richard to read his story from the book. The whole time he was reading, he was flooded with tears. It was a story of tears, pain, suffering and faith and is called, "Turning the Page." Richard gained respect from others and he preached many times in worship services. He was an excellent preacher and people were inspired by his teaching.

In one of the worship services, after Richard had preached, I saw a big smile on his face. He said, "Chaplain, I want to follow you wherever you go, and you should have me preach in all the worship services in this facility."

I replied, "Your vision is a great vision. I believe your desire to preach comes from God. However, our facility would not allow maximum inmates to mix with other inmates, but keep praying. God will open the doors for you. Your testimony will go to many places through *Maximum Saints* books. You can reach out to many other people through your story." His testimony was also published in the book: *Maximum Saints Make No Little Plans*.

Richard was effective. One day an inmate from another pod said to me, "Many people knew Richard on the street. He is not the same person anymore. He has changed. Just looking at him carrying the Bible and hearing him talking about God is so encouraging."

One day, Richard said, "Chaplain, I want to be like you." I asked, "In what ways?" He replied, "I want to be a chaplain. I don't have any training, but God told me that I will not serve as a prisoner but as a minister."

I have met a few who have said that they wanted to be ministers, but Richard was more serious than anyone I had ever met. I believe God called him to be a minister. He had experienced the leading power of God to be a minister to others who are incarcerated. He just did not have the title, but in God's eyes I believe he is a chaplain for other prisoners.

In 2010, between the other chaplain and myself, we have led 24 worship services every week and eight of them are maximum inmates' worship services. Worship services are one of the highest priorities on my list because I have seen the Holy Spirit's powerful movement in them. When people experience God's overwhelming love and conviction of the Holy Spirit, they can't help but change. Worship services provide that opportunity for inmates to experience the transforming power of the Holy Spirit. There is no change in a person's behavior until his or her heart is changed. Therefore, I am so grateful for Richard and Mr. Fuller for their efforts to make maximum inmates' worship possible.

Before Richard left ACDF, he handed me 196 pages of his testimony. He told me after he had read my book *Journey With Jesus*, he was inspired to write his story. When I started working on *Maximum Saints Forgive* book, God reminded me of Richard's story and I knew God was asking me to add his story. His story is a gift to many who are in need of hope, forgiveness, and direction in life.

Many of Mr. Smittal's stories are published in different *Maximum Saints* books and this story is published in the book *Maximum Saints Forgive*, and titled "A Discovery of Maximum Saints" and his testimony is titled "A Messenger."

10. "FINDING HOPE" — Jason Vigil and Michah Collins

I met Jason after a traumatizing event. His wife, Marla, had overdosed and passed away. I had no words to comfort this young man. I was thinking, "What could help him? The only thing that will help him is to bring her back." My heart was heavy whenever I thought about him and his grief.

Months passed and the next time I saw him was at the medical unit. He sent a kite (request) to see me. This time when I saw him, he was not the same person. He came out with a grin on his face. He was smiling. I couldn't believe it. The last time I saw him, he looked so sad. I saw how his heart was broken from losing his wife.

He said, "Chaplain, do you remember me?" I replied, "Of course I do." He said, "This book changed my life." He put the book, *Maximum Saints Never Hide in the Dark* on the table. He said, "I was concerned about my wife's salvation after she died. I agonized. What if she is in hell? This book tells me that before she died, someone led her to the Lord while she was at ACDF. I can see her someday in heaven. I kept two books so I can take them out of the facility."

I never thought I would see Jason smile, but in a short time, he was filled with joy. His wife was saved and he would see her someday. He showed me many poems of how he has hope now since Marla is in heaven. This gave me chills and even tears as I thought about what God can do and what saints at ACDF can do. I was very encouraged.

Jason's transformation was obvious. Instead of getting depressed and staying in grief and pain, he started ministering to others. Jason's story is published in the book, *Maximum Saints Make No Little Plans,* and it is titled "Discovery of Maximum Saints" and his testimony is titled, "Yes, Jesus Loves Me."

I was so encouraged. I said to myself, "Many people worked hard for this book, and if all the hard work was done only for Jason, it was worth it." I also remember Rosemae, who introduced Jesus to Marla, and Michah who helped Jason. Rosemae and Michah were leading Bible studies in their own pods, and both were powerful leaders. I am so thankful for these saints. Here is Michah's story.

"MY TESTIMONY" by Michah Collins

I want to share with you how God has used me, not only in the Adams County Jail, but also in many other institutions in the State of Colorado. But first, I'd like to tell you a bit about my background.

I was born in Fort Scott, Kansas, a small country town, on August 22, 1974. When I was seven years old, my father was murdered. He became my mother's deceased husband, and I was a fatherless child. Upon losing her husband, my mother fled to Colorado to escape the horror and memory of such a tragedy.

My father's death had a powerful impact on me. At eleven years of age, while searching for a father figure, I was led into drugs and gang violence I have a very dark past and was in and out of group homes. At the age of fourteen, I was charged as an adult in bad company and became the youngest person in the state of Colorado to serve time in the Department of Corrections.

I can remember crying, and looking out my prison window when I was sixteen; wondering what all the other sixteen year olds in the world were doing. I had to fight for my life — being the youngest inmate out of a thousand men in Canyon City. I experienced some horrible things behind those prison bars.

I began to hear God's call and got saved in prison at seventeen years of age. After that, although I continued to be in and out of prison, God chose to use me in a mighty way. Eventually, I came to ACDF where I was classified as maximum on January 3rd, 2005. At that time, the maximum people didn't get to have church. I prayed that we maximum people could have church. God's response was, "That's what I have you here for." I began to lead a Bible study in our pod and watched men's lives changed by the power of God.

After three months, I bonded out. After a year's time, I lost at trial and was returned to the Adams County Jail. But, here's the miracle: I came back to the same pod, the same cell, and the same bed, only to see that God was still moving in B Module, Pod 3. Other maximum saints were praying and doing the work of God in my absence. As I watched men's lives being changed, a young man named Jason Vigil moved into my cell. I heard God's voice say, "He's one of mine, and there is work to be done." As our relationship began to grow, I was able to minister to him. He mentioned his girlfriend, Marla Rose, who lost her life from a drug overdose. He wondered if she had made it to heaven.

One day, when the book, *Maximum Saints Never Hide in the Dark*, came to us, I opened it up to a page that said, "A Friend Named Marla." Right away I heard Jason's name in my mind, so I took the book to him and said, "Read this." Minutes later, he came to me, crying. Lo and behold, it was the story of Marla Rose. Another maximum saint had introduced Marla to Jesus, and she had given her life to God. Though Marla lost her life, she also was released from jail and is now free. I tell this story so that you might look at the awesome power of God. After all, when Jason knew where his Marla is resting, he began to ask me questions about God. And now, he's another one who has been won for the kingdom.

Mr. Collins' story is published in the book, *Maximum Saints Make No Little Plans*.

11. "GOD CAN FORGIVE ANYONE" — Samuel Uribe

Samuel was nine or ten years old when he gave his life to Christ. His father had just gotten out of prison and introduced Christ to him. This young boy later didn't think God was real. At the age of 14, he turned to a destructive life style and smoking marijuana. At the age of 16, he joined a gang and dropped out of school. Making matters worse, he was using cocaine, stealing cars, robbing houses, people, and committing many other crimes. He didn't care but he knew he was doing wrong.

He started calling on Satan. He had encounters with Satan who promised him all the things in life that he wanted. Satan said, "God don't love you. If he did, he would give you what you want. Why do you suffer? But I love you. I will give you whatever you want. All you have to do is give me your star and fight with me at the final battle. If you sell me your soul, you will live until that day, plus I'll make you rich, give you the finest women, and everyone will fear you."

Samuel made a contract with the devil that day. He got into witchcraft and black magic, while communicating with Satan. He became very violent and obsessed with death. He thought he was a demon, that he could not die. Then one day a man handed him a tract saying, "Did you know Jesus has the power to rip up that contract you signed with Satan?" And it also said that no matter what he had done, if he asked God to forgive him, He will be forgiven.

He was still running away from the Lord. Then the Lord spoke to him, "Stop running from me. I do love you and I want to show you the truth." God reminded him that he was the Lord and the contract he made with Satan had no power. He was offering salvation.

Finally, Samuel confessed his sins and asked for forgiveness. When he was incarcerated, he wrote his testimony of how he was growing in the Lord.

"IT DOESN'T MATTER WHAT YOU HAVE DONE, GOD WILL FORGIVE YOU" by Samuel Uribe

On May 1, 2006, I turned myself in. As I was being booked in, I was told I was denied work release by the jail. I felt God had a different plan for me. I said a prayer, "God, I know I've been going back to my old ways. I know I'm dirty. I know I can do nothing without you. I know I've put other things above you. Please make me clean. I need help. I can't do it on my own. I know you are in charge, and I trust you. Do what you have to do to make me the man you want me to be."

When I got to my pod, I read a couple of books but could never get into them. Then I picked up another book. The cover was missing. I turned to the middle and read. It was a story about a man who knew the Lord, fell away, came to jail and found the Lord again. Only now, he really knows Him on a whole new level. This book had other stories of pain, struggle, survival and most importantly, victory, victory through Christ. The name of that book is *Maximum Saints Never Hide in the Dark* It gave me the encouragement to live for Christ. I mean really live, not just fifty per cent but one hundred per cent. It made me realize that I have to surrender to Christ to really know Him, just like when I turned myself in. I surrendered.

I now know in order for me to really know Jesus, I must be willing to deny myself all the fleshly things of this world. Things really aren't important. Just as God sacrificed His only Son, I also must make a sacrifice — myself! God's Word says, *"You will seek me and find me when you seek me with all your heart."* (Jeremiah 29:13) I want to find God. I want that relationship. I remember before I just wanted His blessings, but now, I just want Him. Without Him, everything else is meaningless! Remember, it doesn't matter what you've done. Our Lord will forgive you because of what Jesus did on the Cross. The devil is a liar! Jesus is the Truth, the Light, and the Way. The only Way! *"Therefore, I urge you, brothers, in view of God's mercy, to offer your bodies as living sacrifices, holy and pleasing to God – this is your spiritual act of worship. Do not conform any longer to the pattern of this world, but be transformed by the renewing of your mind. Then you will be able to test and approve what God's will is – his good, pleasing and perfect will."* (Romans 12:1-2)

Samuel temporarily became the chaplain's trusty. He shared his testimony in many modules. His powerful story touched many people. In one of the worship services he was reading his testimony in tears the whole time. After he finished reading, everyone got up from their seats and applauded for more than a minute. This has never happened. Samuel was very encouraged and his testimony was published in the book, *Maximum Saints Make No Little Plans*.

12. "ANOINTED TOUCH" — Mireya Vizcarra

When I started working as a chaplain at ACDF in 2003, there was no Hispanic ministry. Our facility didn't even have Spanish Bibles available. I called Sara Choi, a Korean woman, and she donated $500 to purchase Spanish Bibles. Some churches also donated Spanish Bibles, and since then, we have been able to provide Spanish Bibles. Our facility had English worship services and Bible studies, but there were no programs for Hispanic inmates. Hispanic inmate leaders reminded me that they needed worship services and Bible studies to grow in faith. I didn't know what to do since I couldn't speak Spanish.

Transformation Project was producing only English books up to that time. Hispanic leaders requested *Journey With Jesus* in Spanish. I told them it wasn't available in Spanish, but they could translate it. Three Hispanic leaders in Module F began translating the book. I was deeply moved by the concern and dedication of the Hispanic leaders to help their own people and by their enthusiasm about translating the book. With the help of the inmates, I started gathering people for Spanish Prayer and Meditation in five different modules. Eventually, I recruited Hispanic pastors from the outside to lead Catholic and Protestant worship services. Our facility now provides seven Spanish language worship services every week. In 2007 alone, Hispanic worship attendance averaged 246 monthly, and the total attendance was 2,948.

The translation of *Journey With Jesus* was a long process. The three inmates working on it left our facility; but another inmate came along to help me. One day during lockdown when all the lights were off, I walked into F Module to see the translator. Sunlight came through the window on the far side of the room, but I didn't think it was bright enough to read. I found this man sitting by a small desk, translating my book, *Journey With Jesus*, in the dim light.

I couldn't believe it. I was so touched by his kind heart. He was helping me to help others. This man completed the translation. Finally, we received funding for this project and TPPM was able to print 20,000 copies of Spanish books.

I am thankful for the Hispanic leaders who convinced me that they desperately needed God and needed spiritual growth. In 2010, I have been blessed with others who could help me with editing, especially the Spanish translation. There have been many editors but I would like to mention one person who has helped me to edit *Twisted Logic, The Shadow of Suicide*.

One day Mireya Vizcarra from F 1400 approached me and told me she could help me with Spanish editing. I told her *Twisted Logic* has been sitting because I couldn't find anyone to finish the final editing. She said she would do it and she did a great job. She later wrote a testimony and I had to laugh because God wants to help more people, so He was speaking to her. I was very encouraged.

"ANOINTED TOUCH" by Mireya Vizcarra

Being a part of Transformation Project Prison Ministry (TPPM) wasn't my plan at all, but God's. *"You did not choose me, but I chose you and appointed you to go and bear fruit-- fruit that will last. Then the Father will give you whatever you ask in my name."* (John 15:16) I am excited to be a part of TPPM, knowing that my work will affect others in a positive way; it will help others spiritually. I personally believe that God's power has no limits. This is the reason I will not be surprised to see TPPM reaching out across the nation and even around the world. *Maximum Saints* stories have a greatly anointing touch and are encouraging. Reading them helped me to understand God's love and helped me to learn to love Him and love others as well. *"Jesus replied: 'Love the Lord your God with all your heart and with all your soul and with all your mind.' This is the first and greatest commandment. And the second is like it: 'Love your neighbor as yourself.'"* (Matthew 22:37-39)

Within a month or two of my arrest, I noticed people were helping Chaplain McDonald to edit Maximum Saints books. It had true stories, testimonies of how people have been finding God in the midst of darkness. *"God did this so that men would seek him and perhaps reach out for him and find him, though he is not far from each one of us."* (Acts 17:27) When we are experiencing situations without hope, with no one to help us, we feel exhausted and overwhelming. This is when we turn to God, crying out to Him. *"Come to me, all you who are weary and burdened, and I will give you rest. Take my yoke upon you and learn from me, for I am gentle and humble in heart, and you will find rest for your souls. For my yoke is easy and my burden is light."* (Matthew 11:28-30)

God is always with us. He is patiently waiting for the moment we would begin to seek Him. Now He is full of joy and smiling because we are seeking Him. *"I tell you that in the same way there will be more rejoicing in heaven over one sinner who repents than over ninety-nine righteous persons who do not need to repent."* (Luke 15:7) *"In the same way, I tell you, there is rejoicing in the presence of the angels of God over one sinner who repents."* (Luke 15:10) Even torment He would turn into a blessing. This was the opportunity that God was waiting for.

At first, when I noticed other people helping the chaplain, I said to myself, "Not me!" I don't want to compromise my time, getting out of my comfort zone. I thought I was doing enough: reading the Bible, going to Bible studies, fasting for my spiritual growth and praying for my children. Chaplain McDonald gave me Prayer Project Brochures and they were a powerful tool and very helpful in my journey of spiritual growth. So, I was thinking God knew how much I was doing. Why would He want me to do more than that? Why should I do it? That was enough and that was my wrong thinking. God's word showed me differently. *"Then he said to his disciples, 'The harvest is plentiful but the workers are few.'" (Matthew 9:37)*

I was resisting and I was experiencing constant conviction because I knew a gentle voice was talking to me. I was being disobedient to God. I didn't have a choice but to follow what the Holy Spirit was pointing me to do.

The amazing part is, obeying God blesses us. We are blessed abundantly even more than we can ever imagine. *"When he had finished speaking, he said to Simon, 'Put out into deep water, and let down the nets for a catch.' Simon answered, 'Master, we've worked hard all night and haven't caught anything. But because you say so, I will let down the nets.' When they had done so, they caught such a large number of fish that their nets began to break." (Luke 5:4-6)* *"He said, 'Throw your net on the right side of the boat and you will find some.' When they did, they were unable to haul the net in because of the large number of fish." (John 21:6)*

I thought, "I am helping the chaplain to help others." While I was helping her, I was the one who was blessed the most. Wow! I was planting seeds without even realizing it. *"But the one who received the seed that fell on good soil is the man who hears the word and understands it. He produces a crop, yielding a hundred, sixty or thirty times what was sown."* (Matthew 13:23)

My involvement helped me to understand the depths of other people's pain and suffering. Other people have been hurt in many different ways, as much as I was. If others and I were healed with God's love, everybody can be healed. This is the good news that He has commanded me to share. *"The Spirit of the Lord is on me, because he has anointed me to preach good news to the poor. He has sent me to proclaim freedom for the *prisoners and recovery of sight for the blind, to release the oppressed, to proclaim the year of the Lord's favor." (Luke 4:18-19)*

God's love is within reach for all of us in the same way. He loves us all the same. Moment by moment I grow spiritually. Between my involvement in TPPM, Chaplain McDonald and many other beautiful people that have been mentoring me, I am getting stronger and stronger in my relationship with God. And, of course, God's grace helped me in understanding and knowing my creator. Because His love and mercy is great, He chose me. *"You did not choose me, but I chose you and appointed you to go and bear fruit-- fruit that will last. Then the Father will give you whatever you ask in my name." (John 15:16)*

He has been planning this time for me to be used wisely. This has been my "wilderness place" and opened my senses to the maximum. *"If any of you lacks wisdom, he should ask God, who gives generously to all without finding fault, and it will be given to him." (James 1:5)* I have been learning how to rely on Him, how great His love is. I am listening to His voice tell me why I should be obedient and how powerful He is. Even when I am in the midst of problems, He blesses me with His power and peace. *"I have told you these things, so that in me you may have peace. In this world you will have trouble. But take heart! I have overcome the world." (John 16:33)*

He is with me even when I do not feel it. When I listen and obey Him, I feel unexplainable joy and I can't stop smiling, thinking He is looking at me. I know being obedient pleases Him. Now, I know, in every evil temptation, He will turn it into a blessing. God's power is incomparable. He is just asking me to keep my faith in Him through any difficult time. He will give me strength and bless me and then go and help others. *"Simon, Simon, Satan has asked to sift you as wheat. But I have prayed for you, Simon that your faith may not fail. And when you have turned back, strengthen your brothers." (Luke 22:31-32)*

It has been over a year that I've been here. But because of His grace, I am content. It's not about time, place or luxury. That doesn't matter. What is really important is God. *"I am not saying this because I am in need, for I have learned to be content whatever the circumstances. I know what it is to be in need, and I know what it is to have plenty. I have learned the secret of being content in any and every situation, whether well fed or hungry, whether living in plenty or in want. I can do everything through him who gives me strength."* (Philippians 4:11-13)

Now I understand why He created me and what I should be doing, and why I need to go through suffering in life. *"'We must go through many hardships to enter the kingdom of God,' they said."* (Acts 14:22b) I used to be running in life like I was in a race, but I didn't know where it started or where it will end. Now I know where I came from and where I am going – to my heavenly and eternal home. Praise and all glory to my king, my only God! Forever I will love you.

This story will be published in the book *Maximum Saints All Things Are Possible* and her other story, "Empty" was published in the book, *I Was The Mountain*. Her dream story was published in the book, *Dreams and Interpretations, Healing from Nightmares*. Also, her testimony will be coming out in the *Maximum Saints* DVD which will be in English and Spanish.

13. "GOD IS REAL" — Lakiesha Vigil

I have many people helping me with the editing of the *Maximum Saints* books and my books. From time to time, God sent me different special people to help me edit the book. I have many people who worked hard but I would like to mention one special person who did so much work for me.

Ms. Vigil was more enthusiastic about the book project than anyone I had ever met. She helped me with editing and also helped others to write by writing the story for them for the book project.

When God asked me to go back and rewrite my book, *Journey of Mystical Spiritual Experiences*, I wasn't willing. Many of the stories were already published in *Dreams and Interpretations*. Ms. Vigil compared my two books, so I would avoid lots of repetition in the new book. Finally, with her help, I was able to write a new book called, *I Was The Mountain, In Search of Faith and Revival*.

One day when I went inside her pod to lead a prayer, she wanted to talk to me alone. We went to the contact room and she shared how she had a dream of meeting Jesus. She lost her son and Jesus let her know that he was okay. "God is real," she said. She then wrote a powerful testimony about her encounter with God.

She is young, only 21 years old, facing lots of time. So she was wondering if she could continue with the book project when she gets to Denver Women's Correctional Facility (DWCF) after she is sentenced. But DWCF does not have the book project. I encouraged her to write her own book and contact churches on the outside and ask them if they can help her to publish it. Here is a part of her life story.

"AMAZING DREAMS" by Lakiesha Vigil

I got housed in D Module after I talked to the chaplain. At this point I was in total shock. I was numb. I couldn't eat or sleep. I couldn't feel or think. I was just stuck. I read the book, *Maximum Saints Never Hide in the Dark*. As I read all the stories, I stopped and thought, " God really loves me!" I started attending Bible studies. I read my Bible every night and I prayed. I thought that was all I needed to feel peace. Boy, was I wrong!

Now let's get to the good part. January 25, 2011, I had the most beautiful, amazing dream ever. I was praising God, singing for Him in Spanish. Giving Him the glory He deserves. I was on a hill with green grass, big trees, beautiful flowers, and birds flying in the sky. It was an awesome view. I'd seen this incredibly handsome man dressed in a white robe. Remember I told you about losing my son? Okay, well, this man planted a seed in the ground. I watched it grow into a tall pretty flower. That seed was my son. As this flower grew I heard an angelic voice say to me, "Everything will be okay."

If you haven't guessed by now that man was none other than Jesus Christ. He let me see that my son is okay and grew up to be a handsome little angel. The Lord said Himself; everything will be okay. He gave me the honor to see Him face to face. He is real!

I believe He gave me this dream so I could put my trust in Him. This was His way of telling me not only is He real, He has the power to heal a broken heart. Like a real father, He was there to pick up His daughter when she fell and healed her scrapes.

I believe God is going to use Ms. Vigil with her powerful testimony of how God can bring healing. When there was a suicide in the facility, unfortunately she was the one who found her roommate hanging. Eventually her roommate died and it shook Ms. Vigil. She is taking medication to help her with the shock and pain she is going through because of the incident that happened.

When I first heard that Ms. Vigil was the roommate to the woman who hung herself, I was in shock. I asked, "Why Lord, why her? Why did it have to be her?" God only knows. Finding a roommate hanging without warning was not what she had expected. I believe God is going to use her to reach out to many who are in pain and suffering. He uses all our pain and suffering.

Her story is published in my book, *Dreams and*

Interpretations, Healing from Nightmares and will be published in the next book, *Maximum Saints All Things Are Possible*. She also wrote another story about her roommate who committed suicide. It is called, "*The Apple of His Eye.*" Also, her testimony will be coming out in the *Maximum Saints* DVD which will be in English and Spanish.

14. "NO LONGER SERVE SATAN" — Timothy Garcia

When I first met Timothy Garcia, he told me he had decided to believe in Jesus. His body was covered with tattoos and he was really excited about attending chaplain's worship services.

He got baptized, when I gave him the Baptism certificate, he said, "I didn't know that you are the one who wrote *Maximum Saints* books." I replied, "Actually, inmates wrote them. I just gathered their stories and made them into books."

His testimony was unbelievable. He used to be a devoted Satan worshiper, and got into a lot of trouble. He was suicidal when he learned that he may again go to prison this being the fifth time. He said that he worshipped and loved Satan. He had an intimate relationship with Satan. Satan had promised him many good things, but what he got was more prison sentences.

After he got out of the suicide observation unit, he started reading *Maximum Saints* books and found the Lord. That's how he decided to come to worship services. He told me that he used to worship Satan and had a relationship with him. The demons were attacking him after he decided to follow Jesus, but he knew how to fight the demons with the power of Jesus. He prays all day, reads the Bible and is winning the battle by relying on Jesus and putting on the full armor of God. He said he will try to go to school to be a minister after he is released.

He shared how he used to be violent and destructive before he found the Lord. But since he gave his life to Christ, he started sharing Christ with others.

He told me how his satanic tattoos bothered him after he became a Christian. I told him that instead of getting bothered by it, he can use it to reach out to others who are worshipping Satan and those who are searching in the wrong places. He could use that to tell others how God changed him.

Mr. Garcia gave a testimony of how he turned to the Lord. He is also warning young people of the dangers of following Satan. His story was published in the *Maximum Saints Walk into the Light* DVD and also, *Maximum Saints Dream* book and is titled, "I Serve the Lord."

He was preaching in worship services and was helping others, especially those who used to worship Satan or other gods. With his spiritual knowledge about Satan, he was able to help others who are suffering from demonic attacks.

15. "ALL THINGS ARE POSSIBLE" — Heather Lopez

Heather Lopez is an incredible leader. She had been helping me with the editing of the books and leads the prayer meeting in the pod whenever she can.

"ALL THINGS ARE POSSIBLE" by Heather Lopez

My dad and brother got raided when I was 12 years old. The F.B.I. and D.E.A. were on my roof and surrounded the house one night when I came home from roller skating. My dad and brother went to prison when I was 13 years old. My dad got a ten year Federal Prison sentence. My brother was 17 years old and he got a five year Federal Prison sentence for transporting methamphetamines across state lines. I was so lost after they took my dad. My mom lost everything and my other brother pawned all of my dad's expensive things. I ended up running away all the time and was in and out of jail by the age of 13. The judge and my mom said I was a threat to myself and society. Here I am, 13 years old, with theft, joyriding, car theft, assault and battery, escape, drinking under age and lots more.

My husband and I met when I was 11 years old. He was my best friend's brother. I married him when I was 15 years old and he was 29 years old. I have three beautiful kids by him, 4, 9 and 13 years old, two girls and a boy. They are my pride and joy. He gave me three angels out of the whole horrible relationship.

During 2005, he got out of prison. I was in a halfway house. We were together for the first time and I went to Denver Women's Correction Facility (DWCF). I found out as soon as I got there that I was pregnant. While I was in prison, I was full term and slipped in the bathroom. I asked to go to medical but it took three days. I was bleeding and leaking fluid. By the time they saw me, my baby, Mikey, had died. I was in labor for 48 hours because he was dead. He wasn't moving down the birth canal. The pain I was in, and the hate I had in my heart was so strong, it was indescribable — not to mention I was handcuffed and shackled the whole time. I got to hold him as blood was coming out of his nose and mouth.

When they took him away from me, I stated that I would be okay. When something bad happens, I resort back to using drugs and alcohol. I began using meth when I was 15 years old. I went from snorting, to smoking to I.V. using. I never thought it could happen to me. I met my boyfriend in March and he brought me back to church and to the Lord. I felt the Holy Spirit in me that day. On January 5, 2010, we went to steal, everything went wrong, and I am sitting here facing 16 to 32 years.

Now, here I am and even though it sounds bad, I am okay because I have God and His son with me. They are carrying me right now. I have learned that without God, my world was out of control and unmanageable. I had to let go of my resentment, hurts, worries, angers, and twisted logic. I thank God for all the Christians He put in my life. God has given me the strength to go through my struggles and get through all the pain. I am smiling now. I still struggle with pain and nightmares. I rebuke Satan in the name of Jesus. My pain and tears will dry up. Nightmares are from my PTSD. My meds are helping, but what helps me more is prayer. God makes them go away.

One day Ms. Lopez showed me her daughter's letter and she was flooded with tears. It's difficult for her to be away from her family, especially her children. Life has been hard for her but she tells me that she sings and prays with her daughter on the phone. Also, she tries to find Bible verses everyday and writes them in the letters so her daughter can learn about God. She is trying to plant the seed of faith in her children's hearts even though she is incarcerated.

Mrs. Lopez's story is published in the book, *I Was The Mountain* also in the book *Maximum Saints All Things Are Possible*.

16. "A HAPPY RABBIT" — Crystal Gillespie

Crystal was a young woman who had the brightest smile. In F 1400, she was always helping others in the pod trying to cheer everybody up.

However, she wasn't like that when she first arrived at ACDF. The first time I heard about Crystal was from a pod deputy who was concerned about this young woman who was going around the whole pod doing spells. I didn't know who Crystal was at the time.

Not long after that, something happened to Crystal.

She somehow got a hold of Rick Warran's book *The Purpose Driven Life*, and started reading it. At first she tried to check out what Christianity was about then slowly she started changing. She was convinced that God was real because of this book. In no time, she became a Christian and she became a very positive influence.

Crystal started joining prayer meetings when I went inside the pod. That's when I started noticing her bright smile. She started sharing with others how she used to be a devoted wiccan, but she wasn't happy until she found God. She finally found peace and joy after she became a Christian. Her change was noticed, even by deputies.

One day when I went to F 1400, Crystal was wearing bunny make up on her face and had bunny ears on her head. She wiggled a little bunny tail made out of socks and that was really cute. She told me her pod got into trouble that there was no TV privilege. Everyone was getting so bored and restless. She did a play for the whole pod many times to cheer them up. The deputy in the pod mentioned to me that Crystal was doing a great job cheering others up.

I asked her if I could watch her play. She was so excited and said, "Come and I will gather others to play it for you." I sat and watched how Crystal was jumping around like a bunny and picking up different paper bags others had put in different places. It was short and it was great to see how she could be so creative to make other people laugh in a gloomy place. Crystal had a gift of encouragement and brought humor to brighten others' hearts. She certainly did it for me that day.

After my husband died in a car accident in 2008, God brought healing into my heart within three months. I didn't grieve any more. It was a miracle. I was able to minister to inmates. One day Crystal said, "Chaplain, you are an inspiration to all of us. You have gone through a lot, suddenly losing your husband. When we see you smiling that really encourages us."

Here again, Crystal was encouraging me. She was using her gifts to the maximum. Whenever she opens her mouth, she is encouraging someone. She truly was a blessing to many people while she was at ACDF, including myself. Her story is coming out in the book, *Maximum Saints All Things Are Possible* and is titled "He Never Gave Up On Me."

17. "DANCING FOR THE LORD" — Donna Tabor

Donna was six months old when her uncle killed her mother with a brick. Growing up in an orphanage, she thought sex was love and having drugs was a way to handle pain in life. Then she met God who told her He loved her. From then on Donna experienced healing in her heart and she has great love for the Lord. She had a tough life from abusive relationships and had to let her children be adopted. She still shines with a big smile and is very positive in the maximum pod. She knows God gives her that joy even in incarceration.

She has faith and the knowledge of the Scripture so others look up to her to hear her. At some point, I noticed that she wasn't smiling. She told me she was praying to get her joy back because somehow she lost it. Whenever I went inside the pod, her prayer request was asking for joy from the Lord.

One day when she again shared that her prayer request was to have joy back, I said, "There are many ways you can lose joy. See if any of the things I describe would fit in your case. First, check how your mind works: you will lose joy if you spend 90 % of your time on worrying and spend only 10% time with God.

Second, see how you spend time: if you spend time and focus 90% of your time on something else and spend

10% of your time reading the Bible or praying, you will lose joy.

Third, see if you think about what God has done for you: if your focus is on what you don't have, and you forget what God gave you, you will lose joy.

Fourth, see if you are serving the Lord: if you focus on finding joy only for yourself and do not focus on helping others to find joy, you will lose joy because you are selfish.

Fifth, watch what you say: if you don't proclaim what you have in Christ, you will lose joy. So, instead of focusing on what you don't have which is joy at this point, start proclaiming what you have received and have in Christ.

If I were you, I would walk around and pray until you find joy in Christ. Each step, you can say, "I have joy because I have Jesus. I have joy because I am saved. I have joy because the Holy Spirit is with me. I have joy because God cares for me, etc. You can also dance for joy while proclaiming joy."

Donna followed my suggestions. She started, jumping, dancing even stretching and proclaiming joy. Instantly, she was filled with joy. She had so much joy that she didn't have to pray for joy. She had it. The next day when I visited the pod, I asked Donna if she needs to pray for joy. She said, "No, I already have it." I saw her bright smile and she was filled with the Holy Spirit.

About a week later, I saw Donna through the glass on the door as I was talking with a deputy. Donna was jumping and smiling and waving her hands to me. I spoke to her through the crack in the door, "Can you dance for me?" Donna started dancing with a big smile. I was smiling and the deputy was smiling. She found joy. I was so happy that she was able to proclaim what she needed. She needed the strength through joy. God gave her joy.

Donna is an anointed servant of God and gifted with

prayer and songs. Many expressed how thankful they are when they are with Donna. When she opens her mouth, the words are precious. When she prays, she is a preacher.

The most inspiring anointed worship I have ever felt in the whole facility so far is with Donna and another woman, Vesta Hight. In worship, Donna sings beautiful songs for the Lord. I am so touched by her love for the Lord. One kneels and is falling on the floor in reverence to the Lord. The other one is speaking in tongues, praising Jesus and is dancing. The Holy Spirit blesses all of us.

I've never experienced the strong presence of the Lord in worship anywhere else. Actually it happens in different modules at different times with certain inmates. In Worship, I've never felt that much anointing of the Holy Spirit then when I worship in D Module with maximum saints. The Lord blesses people who truly worship God, and that's Donna and Ms. Hight.

On Sunday May 22, Donna and Ms. Hight and Lisa Newberry did a skit in the worship service. Donna was holding a Bible and reading it to Ms. Hight, who was a gangster in the play. Ms. Newberry made sarcastic remarks saying Jesus was not for Ms. Hight. Donna's persuasion won and Ms. Hight started singing and dancing her testimony as a gangster turned into a Christian. It was powerful. I was amazed by their creativity. I asked two deputies in that module if they would like to come and watch these ladies play. They both came up and watched the play. The deputies were so impressed and said, "You should all do it for the whole pod."

I was so blessed by these three women. When I went inside their pod, I asked them to do the skit for the whole pod and they did. Everyone applauded afterward. They brought smiles to many faces.

I explained what these women did in other pods and

another pod developed a similar skit to perform in their own pod. I can almost see Jesus smiling for what these ladies are doing. It was Donna's idea to make this skit. She said some of her family members go to prisons, do skits and minister. Donna's story was published in my book, *The Ultimate Parenting Guide and* also will be in the *Maximum Saints All Things Are Possible* and is called, "The Lessons."

18. "HE WAS SAD TO LEAVE JAIL" — Greg Lisco

Greg Lisco was an excellent preacher in A Module. Whenever I led Chaplain's worship service, he couldn't wait to preach. He was in medium pod, but he wrote more sermons than anyone I had seen. In his testimony, he shared that he attended church since he was little but he didn't have the relationship with the Lord until he was 31 years old. He wrote:

"IN HIS MAJESTIC SERVICE" by Greg Lisco

I was first introduced to Jesus in the Jefferson County jail. There I met a man who was there on a murder charge. He was a gang member and had been involved in the brutal murder of a young woman. What got my attention was his devotion and the persistence with which he was representing what he called the Gospel.

He told me that he was facing the death penalty for his involvement in this murder. He told me that he had made a deal with God. That if God would spare his life, he would commit to Him to preach the gospel behind bars.

He told me, "For all have sinned, and come short of the glory of God." (Romans 3:23) He told me that the wages of sin is death but the gift of God is eternal life.

I would brush him off and argue with him. "How do you know God wrote that book?" I would say to him. You see what I know now is that the appointed time had come, that all the prayers of my mom and her friends, all the prayers of my grandma and her church were coming to fruition right there in that jail. What I did not know was that a man of God was on his knees in his cell, pleading with God on my behalf. He watered the seed of faith, praise God. He opened my eyes. My friends prayed with me and I accepted Jesus. Who knew that God would take that very thing Satan sent to destroy you, and turn it around for your own good. Isn't life awesome?

I never thought I would see the day I would say that I was sad to leave jail. As I sit here writing this letter, these sad feelings are coming at me again. I know beyond a doubt that I am in the will of God and that even in this dark, dark place, God can and is touching people and changing lives every day. You see that is what the glory of God does. When Jesus shows up, things change. People are healed, the blind see, the lame walk, sins are forgiven and people find out the devil has no claim to them.

I thank and praise God every day that He has chosen me as one of the vessels. He will use me to reach people and to touch people. I am living proof that God's Word does not return to Him void.

That is why I say it makes me sad to leave here. I know beyond a doubt that I am doing what God wants me to do. I can honestly say that even if I don't leave here that is all right, too; I know that every day I spend here I will grow closer to my Lord and my God. I also know that every day I spend here I am adding to my treasure in heaven. It makes me sad to leave because I have so much more work to do for God; I can share with the men in here the things I am learning about God. Not knowing when I will leave here has given me a sense of urgency. I know I will leave, but I don't know when. That is the same way it is with our lives. We know God will take His breath from us, but we don't know when.

His story will be published in the next inmates' book, *Maximum Saints, All Things Are Possible.*

19. "A CHAPLAIN'S TRUSTEE" — Peter Nguyen

Our facility chaplains have an assigned trustee who help us set up worship services. It's really interesting to see how different trustees change as they attend chaplains' worship services every week. We don't choose who will be our trustee. Classification people make that decision.

Once we had a trustee named Peter Nguyen. He was of Vietnamese decedent and didn't want to be a trustee. He told me later that he thought all the people who attended church were fake, and God wasn't real. He used to call each of them "Holy Man" and tease them. Others told him that if he resists God, then He will be after him more. He laughed at that, too. Then one day he found out he was assigned as a chaplain's trustee. First he thought someone was messing with his mind, because he was teasing others who attended church but it was true. He wasn't thrilled and tried to find out how he could avoid this duty but he didn't have any choice on the job assignments.

I had no idea that he had so much struggles inside of himself, but he was a hard worker from the beginning. I was very impressed with how he paid attention to all the details of worship.

"I FEEL LIGHTER" by Peter Nguyen

As time went by, I started to read some of Chaplain McDonald's books and listened to what was said in church. I started to like what I was doing as a trustee. So, after 2 or 3 weeks of helping out as a Chaplain Trustee, a janitor named Ed stopped me in the hallway. He asked me to do something for a week. "Listen to the Holy Spirit each night for an hour, and you will hear the Holy Spirit."

Well, 8 or 9 days went by, and one night as I was doing that, listening to the Holy Spirit, I caught myself weeping a lot. So the next day I told Chaplain McDonald what happened. She told me it was the Holy Spirit. From that day on I started to feel lighter and happier, knowing that the Holy Spirit had spoken to me. I even stopped most of my cursing and all of my bad mouthing about the Lord to others.

What got me more motivated in believing is what is going on in A Module Pod3 with the brothers. I feel that they are so powerful that each time I get to help in their group I get happy. Their testimonials were so powerful that they touched me. Now, each day and night I pray to the Lord about everything He has done for me. Especially now that I believe that He is our Savior.

His story will be coming out in the next inmates' book, *Maximum Saints, All Things Are Possible*.

20. "A MAN WAS SAVED" — John King

I am amazed by how many inmate leaders are saving souls and giving hope to many who don't know that there is hope by sharing Christ. I was leading a worship service and a small group of people came to worship. We sat in a circle and a tall man said, "There is a man who doesn't know the Lord and is hurting. I would like to ask him if he would like to accept Christ." He was asking for my permission and I said that will be fine. The man turned to a young man and said, "Brother, you need to turn to Christ. Are you ready to accept Christ? He will help you."

The young man replied, "Yes, I am ready to accept Christ." The tall man asked the man to repeat the prayer of invitation to accept Christ. I was amazed. I didn't know that this young man wasn't a Christian since this was the first time I saw him. But the inmate from his pod knew.

Another time I saw another miracle happen through a man who felt life wasn't worthwhile.

When John King received bad news from his family, he was hurting badly and tried to hang himself in his jail cell. A deputy saved him by untying him just in time. As uniting the man, he prayed to God to save him. Mr. King was thankful for the prayer offered by the deputy.

One day Mr. King wrote his testimony and prepared to preach. The day he preached, there was only one man who was attending worship and listening to Mr. King's sermon.

He described how he was saved when he tried to kill himself and how God has helped him. Here is a part of his sermon:

"THROUGH PRAYER HEALING CAN BE DONE" by John King

Just as little as three months ago, maybe it was four, I was wandering around aimlessly with no direction in my life, hoping somebody would do for me what I could not do for myself. I was addicted to drugs, not taking care of my children and did not work. After praying for some intervention, God answered my prayers and I was brought to ACDF

Since that day, I have been in constant daily conversation with my Heavenly Father. He is guiding me and I have given my life to Jesus completely. Studying God's word and living a Christian lifestyle, I am as happy as I've ever been in my life. I live peacefully and look forward to my future.

Through prayer and with forgiveness I now know what love is and how to love. I am truly blessed and I give all the credit to God for through His Son, Jesus, He has given me a new life. Through prayer healing can be done, so we should be in constant prayer with God through His Son, Jesus, and faith will allow constant healing. If you are out there and want to be healed of any affliction, you might have or are in need of prayer, and want to confess to Jesus Christ as your personal Savior, come forward and receive the Lord and be healed.

As soon as Mr. King finished his words, the man who was sitting got up and walked to the front to give his life to Christ. Mr. King prayed for him to receive Christ.

That was an unforgettable moment for me. If Mr. King had died the night he tried to kill himself, he would not have been preaching and he would not be able to bring people to Christ. I was so encouraged by what God can do when we decide to live for the Lord.

Mr. King's story was published in the book *Maximum Saints Never Hide in the Dark*.

21. "WHY I AM SO HAPPY" — Jose Marquez and Omar Castaneda

Omar Castaneda was a powerful leader. He preached in many Chaplain's worship services and helped many other inmates who needed God. Here is one testimony of how Omar helped Jose Marquez.

"A TRUE STORY OF REVIVAL" by Jose Marquez

When I was on the streets, I dedicated myself to selling drugs, and also to doing other illegal things. I went to church one time, and I answered an altar call. There I accepted Christ. But truly, at that time I didn't know what was going on. I was still the same person. I kept on drinking, using drugs, and even cheating on my wife.

One day, I found out that my wife was cheating on me. I stayed at home to confront her, but she never came home. A voice inside my head was telling me to leave, but I didn't listen. I was so mad that I wouldn't leave. I wanted to know what was going on. At that moment, the police came to arrest me. My wife had called the cops on me, and I ended up in custody at ACDF.

In here, I had problems with an inmate, but we resolved it. Then, one day, I was listening to Spanish music on my headphones and I heard my wife dedicating a song to her lover. I became extremely depressed, and I tried to commit suicide. I tore a sheet and wrapped it as tightly as I could around my neck. My cellmate told the deputy. I ended up in medical housing on suicide watch for a week. In medical, I didn't eat anything, and I also had problems with an inmate there.

Five days into medical treatment, I was in bed. I heard a positive voice in my head that all this was happening for a reason. I thought about my children and doing something positive for my children. In the holding tank, when I went to court, I had a problem with an inmate. He choked me and I fainted. Then, he slammed me on the ground, split my head open, and I ended up in the hospital. After release from the hospital, I ended up in A Module Pod 1, and a brother in Christ started sharing with me the gospel of salvation. I still didn't feel secure about myself. I still thought that my life had no meaning and that not even God could help me. I went to the hole, and I read the book, *A Divine Revelation of Hell*, by Mary Baxter. It was then that I finally came to my senses, both spiritually and mentally.

After I got out of the hole, I kept on going to the Bible studies that brother Omar was having throughout the week. I accepted Jesus as my Lord and Savior. From that point on, I started developing a relationship with God. I started doing my own Bible studies through the mail. *John 3:16* had a great impact on me and *Galatians 4:4-6* helped me. Paul said, "For *through the law I died to the law so that I might live for God. I have been crucified with Christ and I no longer live, but Christ lives in me. The life I live in the body, I live by faith in the Son of God, who loved me and gave himself for me." (Galatians 2:19-20)*

Even though I am a prisoner, God has adopted me as His son through His grace. Now, that my faith grows, I have joy, peace, and serenity that I have found nowhere else. Serving God is not easy. It is hard. But as Paul said, *"Whatever you have learned or received or heard from me, or seen in me – put it into practice. And the God of peace will be with you." (Philippians 4:9)* Now I understand that why I suffered all of this, is so that I would find God, so I would not perish, but have everlasting life.

"DON'T LET ANYTHING STOP YOU FROM SERVING THE LORD" by Omar Castaneda

When I served the devil, I sold drugs. I was a tattoo artist and did body piercing for fifteen years. With all that, I was good. I also had an honest job, but at the same time I was using drugs to the point where we were kicked out of the first three apartments we had. I still didn't stop selling or using them. We ended up at my baby's mom's sister's apartment. There I ended up selling rock, and taking control on that block. Nobody would sell there but me. This went on for a few years. I made a lot of money, so we were able to rent a house. Everything was good — money, house, and family. In 2002, I got a drug charge. I did a deferred sentence, so there was no felony on that. I had a hard time because of selling and using drugs.

April 2004 is when I said, "Lord Jesus, I need you in my life." So, my walk with the Lord started after I accepted Jesus in my life. This was my thought, "I have been serving the devil for fifteen years. Now, I am going to serve God for fifteen years. When these fifteen years go by, I can decide which fifteen years were better: those serving the devil or those serving God."

By October 1, I had lost my house, my family, and had separated from my girlfriend of ten years. We have two daughters together, so she ended up with the little one and I kept the oldest. I lost all the things that we had — movies, CDs, entertainment center, cars, everything. I ended up with nothing but one daughter. Next thing you know, I was staying with my daughter's aunt again. Prior to that, I was in a car accident. I ended up with a blood clot in my lung and three broken ribs. One morning, after I went to get my blood level checked, I took some pain pills and saw my baby's mom's sister coming down the stairs. She told me that her sister's boyfriend beat her. I went to her apartment, and one thing led to another. I defended myself, and I ended up getting a murder charge.

God had a plan for me. I didn't see it. I ran to seek God's guidance. He showed me *2 Samuel 24:12-13*. I had to make a choice to either turn myself in or keep running away. God said, "You are going to preach my word the same way as when you were on the street selling drugs." I said, "My life is in your hands. Let it be so. I know I won't do this alone, for you are with me." I turned myself in.

I am looking at a sentence of life without parole or death. I have been serving God almost two years, and I rejoice daily. Serving Him is all I do. I have touched so many lives. I have helped people coming into jail (who wanted to commit suicide), give their lives to God. I have helped people in distress, anguish, turmoil, and without peace as they have come to me. The Holy Spirit has worked through me. They rejoice and end up with peace in their lives. People ask me why I am so happy in a place like this. I just tell them I have Jesus in my life, and the next thing you know, they want what I have.

I lead three Bible studies every week in our pod, and I thank God for providing me with the knowledge He has given me. I won't trade it for anything. To all those who have a case like mine, and feel that God cannot use them, that's a lie of the devil. Prison is where you get built up. *(Colossians 2:6-7, 2 Timothy 2:19-21)*

Don't let anything stop you from serving the Lord. Like I said, it hasn't been fifteen years yet serving God, but I will tell you right now, I won't go back to serving the devil. *(Revelation 20:10,15)* I'd rather see you all in heaven. *(Revelation 21:3-4)* With all sincerity, and truth, I close this with these words of encouragement: *"So, if the Son sets you free, you will be free indeed." (John 8:36)*

Jose Marquez and Omar Castaneda's stories were published in the book *Maximum Saints Make No Little Plans*.

22. "I THANK JESUS" — Monica Valdez

I met Monica Valdez when she was having a difficult time making a decision whether she should amputate her leg or not. Eventually, she made the decision to amputate her leg. But her faith grew as time passed and I saw her blossom in the worst situation. From a timid, wandering mind to one solid in faith and sharing God with others. She could be falling into self-pity or depressive thoughts if she focused on her leg, but she looked up to Jesus and found comfort.

Ms. Valdez was gifted with visions and dreams and had the passion to serve the Lord. One day she asked me to pray for her and that she wanted to serve Jesus to the fullest. Her focus was on pleasing the Lord and I was very touched and many others were blessed by her testimony.

When a Rocky Mountain Newspaper reporter asked me if I could find a female inmate to interview, immediately God told me to recommend Ms. Valdez. She was in the infirmary at the time. When I asked her if she would like to do an interview with a reporter, she said she would. I asked her to write her testimony so she would be prepared.

A couple hours later, when I went back to see her, she had written many pages of her testimony. She said, "When I started writing my testimony, I felt the Holy Spirit. I am so blessed." When I read her testimony, I was amazed. Her story was anointed. It was a powerful story. She also shared how she was able to see angels when we were talking in the room. She also mentioned that she saw a big angel in a worship service.

When the reporter came out to interview her, we were in the chaplain's office. As she started sharing, I could feel the presence of the Lord so strong and it was a glorious moment I will never forget. She was very eloquent in sharing her story with a stranger who may not quite understand what she was saying.

I was reminded of the Scripture: *"Then those who feared the LORD talked with each other, and the LORD listened and heard. A scroll of remembrance was written in his presence concerning those who feared the LORD and honored his name. 'They will be mine,' says the LORD Almighty, 'in the day when I make up my treasured possession. I will spare them, just as in compassion a man spares his son who serves him. And you will again see the distinction between the righteous and the wicked, between those who serve God and those who do not.'"* (Malachi 3:16-18)

I am very thankful for my encounter with her. I felt so blessed by her ministry at ACDF to many others, including myself. The following is a part of her testimony after someone ran into her car and she was hospitalized and how God blessed her spiritual journey in the midst of pain and suffering.

"I THANK JESUS FOR THIS MOMENT" by Monica Valdez

Three months later I woke up from being in a coma at Denver Health Hospital. All I could remember was a dream of a man walking with me. At first, I was alone in a crazy carnival. As I was walking, all of a sudden I was in a beautiful, peaceful garden. A man was walking by my side, and I was not afraid. He spoke to me and told me I was going to be okay.

When I woke up, I still did not know where I was. I could not walk. Both my legs were broken, my jaw and back were hurt. I had almost bled to death. My leg had been 90% severed and was hanging by the bone. That day I should have died. The paramedics and police were amazed that I was still alive and that the children were not injured. They tried to save my leg. Since no one could give consent to amputate, they left it the way it was, but it was useless.

I spent the next couple of months in the critical-care unit. I was told it would be better to amputate, but I refused. Even then I did not listen to the Lord or thank Him for not letting my soul burn in Hell. I was blessed, and I did not realize how much the Lord was with me. I did not know that through this I would come to the Lord and He would start building me up with His love through my appreciation for not letting me die.

I am just a baby in my faith in Christ, but the more I read *Maximum Saints* books and my Bible, the better I understand. I do not preach yet, but I have received my answer. I asked God to please tell me what to do. He said, "Change your ways. Time is running out. Save yourself and save as many as you can."

My dreams scare me sometimes because I know the spiritual world is real. I see angels in my room, as well as in my dreams. They are the most beautiful amazing things I've ever seen. God is real. Jesus is real. Death is real and so is life.

God has opened my eyes and has even sent me guardian angels. I did not plan this, God did. I will never be the same. This has changed me to believe in the Lord. As I am writing this, there is an angel that stays over me. I can see it clearly. They are not being shy with me. I wish other people could see what I'm seeing. There is a big angel holding the hand of a smaller one. I asked him if I could see them up close, and they were okay with it.

What a blessing for me to see them. I am grateful for this gift, though I question, "Why me?" I know it's because God has made it possible for me to be used as a worker in the harvest and a sister to all God's children. He is going to open a lot of doors. He already has. This moment is what I've lived for. The Lord has prepared me for this so I could witness such an amazing thing and tell people about it. I really feel and know that many people will be saved by my testimony.

I'm starting to understand what my calling is more and more each day. I see these beautiful creations sent not to just some people, but to all. I am just barely realizing how long the Lord has been waiting patiently for me and how much time I wasted. "Father, forgive me. I know you have been there and you still chose to wait. I thank you, Father. Thank you. Lord, you have called me. I will do anything you ask of me. I'm trying to tame the tongue that speaks foul language or deceit." I now know how real all this is, and how I will be used in this spiritual warfare to see angels as well as demons.

I always felt like I did not deserve anything, and I've been so tired of believing in a hopeless life, but I do not feel that way anymore. "God, please do not let me lose my last chance to show my family that I'm changing my life. Jesus, I give you the glory. You gave me the grace. I am nothing without you. Can you see it in my face?"

Ms. Valdez's story was published in the book *Maximum Saints Dream*.

23. "A LIFE SAVED" — Justine Lenzini

I have met many inmate leaders who are more like chaplains to other inmates. Justine Lenzini was one of the leaders with a very soft voice, but she has the message and heart for prisoners. She shared a story one day and I asked her to write her testimony because many people do not realize how much inmates are actually saving lives. She will do anything for you if that will help you, especially if that could save your life. I feel privileged to have gotten to know Ms. Lenzini and I am thankful that she is able to help many others in her pod and I have no doubt that she will be helping many more people while she is incarcerated. Here is her story.

"THANK GOD FOR USING ME" by Justine Lenzini

In January, 1998, I was sentenced to DOC—prison—for 20 years; but that is another story. What happened after that is the testimony I wish to share. See, all of the others who were sentenced around the time I was, had been taken from ACDF to another DOC holding facility within two weeks of their sentencing. It had been almost two months and I was still here. Why? I was a newly born again Christian, hungry to read the Bible and eager to obey God's word. So, I figured there must be a reason for the delay in my move. Still, I was questioning it. Then in early March, as a few of us, who read Scriptures early in the morning were talking about what we read, a woman came in with her box and went into the cell next to mine. No one really paid any attention because this was jail, new people come and go all the time.

Today proved to be different. Within less than half a

minute, the woman came back out. She was upset and very pale. She cried out, "Someone had hung themself in my cell!" I don't recall exactly what my thinking was, but as everyone else ran around yelling for deputies, screaming for help, or running to their own cells to hide; my feet took me straight to the cell with the would be suicide attempt. I had taken CPR and first-aid and was certified at one time, it was expired though. Still, I remembered clearly how to deal with this situation: support the neck and head, remove the "rope" (a sheet in this case), gently lower the victim, check for breathing and perform CPR if necessary. It had been over two years since I'd taken that class, why was it so crystal clear this day? And why hadn't I panicked? I knew I was scared. I can only attest that God had used me to help this woman. I did as I remember, step by step; and as I was about to perform CPR a deputy came in. He said, "I'll take it from here, Ms. Lenzini. You just go lock down." I did as he had told me. Then I did as God told me — I prayed for the young woman who had tried to take her own life. I prayed and I cried for her life as if she were family, when I didn't even know who she was.

About 45 minutes to an hour later, the deputy came to my cell door. He said he wanted to thank me for what I had done, because if the girl had to wait for him there probably her brain would have been damaged, due to the lack of oxygen. Where as, my already having let her down from the tether, she was going to be just fine. I broke down and cried, thanking God for the woman's life. I later found out she was a young mother who's children had been picked up by social services. She thought it was the end of the world. I was told she got counseling and was now happy to be alive.

Now I know that was God's purpose in my delay from leaving ACDF. I say this because I left two days later! Even to this day, I am not certain why I did what I did. I'm not what I would call a brave or even assertive person. And what I recall, to me, seems more like remembering a movie I had watched—like it wasn't me that had done that. I truly believe that the Holy Spirit took over, so I give all glory and praise to God for saving that young woman's life. I thank God for using me, and giving her and her family a second chance at life. I still pray for her and hope she has turned things around.

This experience helped me about a year and a half later, as I felt like my world had come to an end. I was depressed by a letter from my child that hurt me severely. I had wanted to end it all, too. Instead, I cried out to God and He reminded me of the relief everyone in our pod had knowing the woman had survived. They cared. Someone always cares. You may not know who, but there is someone out there who is praying for you. God kept me from attempting suicide that day because I didn't want anyone to find me—like we had found that young girl. I realized then that suicide hurts everyone who comes in contact with it. No one wins, except Satan—who comes to kill, steal and destroy: he kills through suicide; he steals joy and the life that was possible; he destroys all the good that the victims of suicide may have done with their lives.

I have totally turned my life over to God. My 20 year sentence now has less than nine months left to it and I have done that time in service to God. I hope to share more of the testimonies of how He has changed my life for the best and of all He has done for me.

For those who have thoughts of suicide–please, seek out help, even if it's someone who will pray with and for you. Pencils have erasers and nothing is worth letting Satan win even one day of God's precious gift of life. I've heard that many suicide survivors have said they changed their minds after it was too late. They lived to remember that. So, take time to seek help, and you won't go through that. I've also heard that threats of suicide are a cry for help. Take all threats seriously and be part of the solution—even if all you can do is pray, it's what you should be doing! Trust me—I know.

Ms. Lenzini's story will be published in the book, *Maximum Saints All Things Are Possible.*

24. "THE ARTIST" — Charles Polk

We had many wonderful artists for each *Maximum Saints* books, but one person I would like to mention here is Charles Polk. One day I was looking for someone to draw the cover of the *Journey With Jesus*. Mr. Polk took it as an assignment. He drew not only for the cover but he illustrated the book and it has been published. Since then he drew many more pictures and he inspired many others with his drawings.   Mr. Polk told me that before his incarceration, he did lots of other drawings but this was the first time he had tried, but he was amazingly talented and his drawings inspired many people. Here is one of his drawings.

78 / PRISONERS VICTORY PARADE

Drawing "Jesus on the Cross"
By
Charles Polk

Chapter 3

Extraordinary Stories of Former Prisoners:

1. "New Hope Ministries"

Founder, Rev. Ray Chavez

Luther Chavez was a welder and he was hired to put metal bars on the windows at a juvenile Detention Center. One day, he was putting bars on each window including the window where his son, Raymond was. Ray watched him. Dad was outside working hard to provide for his family and Ray was inside with no intention of changing his behaviors. Luther had no intention of bailing his son out either. He believed that you pay the price when you commit crime. Luther grieved for his son's behavior and the punishment didn't change Ray's behavior.

At the age of nine, Ray was devastated and felt lost and indeed he was lost since his mother ran off with another man who worked for his father. His parents divorced and he never guessed or imagined that this would happen to his family. Since then he was ditching school and was on the streets, he got involved in many criminal activities. He was in and out of the Juvenile Detention Center since he was about 14 or 15 years old. Ray was a natural leader instigating criminal activities. He used alcohol and drugs to numb his pain and he had no motivation to change.

No one may have guessed that the boy who was sitting inside the jail and staring at his father would eventually become one of the most effective, spiritual leaders that built a ministry called New Hope Ministries in Lakewood, Colorado. His church is growing. In 2011, on

Sunday morning worship service, approximately 1,200 attend church and 400-500 on Sunday evening and Wednesday night worship.

Pastor Ray Chavez is 61 years old. He and his wife Lola started a church in Denver in 1988, in his apartment. Two people attended. Now this ministry is reaching out to thousands of people. Pastor Ray has been in the ministry for 38 years and he and his wife are the senior pastors of New Hope Ministries. His goal for the ministry is restoration of lives, fathers becoming real fathers and mothers to be real mothers, making Jesus real. He had seen countless people touched by God, delivered from addictions, alcohol, jails, prisons, and bondage. He mentioned that two heroin addicts delivered from addiction became pastors and began ministering to others.

This church is reaching out to so many people hurting from alcohol, drugs, gangs, jail, prisons, homelessness, and broken homes. Pastor Ray understands what these people need and how they can get help and be delivered from pain because he too had experienced what they are going through. Wanting to reach out to those who struggle with addiction, Pastor Ray started a drug rehabilitation center which now houses 50 men and 25 women.

A great spiritual leader and organizer, Pastor Ray's vision is big. His story is published and called, *An Ounce of Hope* and he distributes them free in jails and prisons to reach out to many who are lost and desperately in need of healing and hope in Christ. New Hope Ministry is expanding their ministry. They started a church in Juarez, New Mexico, and churches in Aurora and Thornton, Colorado. His vision is to build churches and ministries in several towns to reach out to many people.

NEW HOPE MINISTRY is located: 5303 W. Kentucky Ave,

Lakewood, CO 80227. Website: www.cohco.org. Their drug rehabilitation is called, Center of Hope: and is a faith based non-profit organization. Jesus can change people's lives. Here is his powerful story of how God brought change in Ray's heart and also how he responded to his call to serve the Lord.

"FINDING HOPE IN CHRIST" by Pastor Ray Chavez

When my older brother Frank got into trouble with the law, he was facing prison sentences. During that time he found God and was freed from all charges. Frank used to take me to church when I was seven or eight years old. My mother came to know the Lord, but later backslid, and that's when she ran off with another man.

My parents were divorced when I was nine years old. It devastated us. We never thought that anything like that could happen to our home. Since then I was on the street. I found acceptance and related to others who were like me, coming from broken homes: Life of alcohol, drug addiction, neighborhood gangs, violence, and destruction.

My father was about 40 years old and he never married again. He didn't want other people to come and abuse his kids. He supported all of us. I was getting in trouble with the law since I was 14 or 15 years old, always in and out of jail. What was lacking in my life was Christ. Drug and alcohol was my life and I kept using them until I lived with my brother Frank.

As a Catholic, we all believed in God but the first time I met God was when I was 21 years old on a train from California to Colorado. I just got out of prison and I was on the way to my brother, Frank's home. He was a pastor in Brighton. The Lord revealed himself to me and I had a vision of my past. God's presence touched my life. God became real to me but I wasn't ready to give my life to Christ at the time.

In 1973, I had a homicide charge from a car accident. A man was killed. I was placed in Adams County Detention Facility (ACDF). The Lord appeared to me and spoke to me, "Ray, if you open the door of your heart, I can set you free." So, I did. That's when God started to change my life. Since then I was delivered from addiction, that was 38 years ago. I had no desire for any alcohol or drugs. If you open the doors of your heart, He will come in, and break the bondage, and deliver you from addiction, alcohol, and drugs.

I stayed a week or two at ACDF and was released on bail. I fought this case, went to trial, appealed it, was found guilty, and they put me back in jail. Again I fought the case for the next two and a half years. Eventually, the Lord set me free. When I was 23 years old, I became a pastor

Frank passed away 13 years ago. My brother Joe never got involved with drugs, he went to a seminary to become a Catholic priest in his late 20's. Then later he became a pastor and went to work with my brother Frank.

Q: Any words to prisoners?

Jesus Christ was an inmate. He was arrested, put in a dungeon and sentenced to death but his purpose was to set prisoners free. He loves them so much that if they call out to him there is not a wall or cell, prison, or law that can keep them away from Jesus. He can change a dope to hope. Jesus has paid the price, you just got to accept.

Q: Any words to families of the incarcerated?

Not to give up hope and faith in God. Keep believing in God because he is a miracle God. Never give up on incarcerated family members. Keep your faith in God. He can help them receive their miracles. Seek the Lord and you will find Him. Ask Him, He moves for you because he loves you. When I was incarcerated, my family never gave up on me.

They prayed for me, encouraged me, visited me and kept believing in God.

Q: Any words to a person who struggles with addiction?
Addiction is a spiritual problem and Jesus Christ can set them free, if they turn to Him with all their heart, He will set them free.

Q: What steps must a person take when they struggle with addiction?
1. Make a commitment in their hearts and mind that the only way out is Jesus Christ.
2. They need to cry out to God.
3. Begin to read the Bible, attend church, begin to grow.
4. Never quit in ups and downs. God is able to change anyone that is willing to trust Him

Q: Do you have any regrets in life?
I have regrets that I have taken a man's life in a car accident. I have hurt others; I should have never hurt them. I hurt others intentionally and unintentionally. I cannot erase those things but God takes our past, regrets, sins and buries them. In the courtroom, I told the family, "I was sorry that this man's life was taken, I wish I could bring him back, but I can't." I wanted to let them know that I was sorry. Two weeks before the accident I was taking drugs, I was getting high. I saw a car coming on the wrong side of the road and I barely missed him. God told me, "You need to give your life to me," but I wasn't ready. Two weeks later, I was in a car accident. If we listen to God, we can prevent lots of grief and pain. Eventually, God healed me from all the hurt and pain.

Q: Have you ministered in prison since you were released?
One night God spoke to me to go to the Adams

County Detention Facility and preach, but I had no desire to minister in jail. To be obedient, I went to the jail and asked a Sergeant, if he needed anyone to preach. He said, "That's the last thing they want to hear." I left it at that, then a week later I got a phone call from a woman and she said, "A young man wants to talk to you." I visited him at ACDF and ministered to him. He was saved and filled with the Holy Spirit. He was incarcerated for murder. He started telling everyone about Christ. ACDF to give me a room to preach, so I was able to preach in jail from 1982 to 1984. Then I quit going to jail to minister when I started revival meetings. In 1988, I met my wife Lola and the Lord called us to be pastors. In 1988 we started a church and we have been ministering for 24 years. Then later many people who came to my church said to me that I ministered to them when they were in prison.

Q: Any miracles that you have experienced that you cannot forget?

One of the greatest things God showed me is God is able to use anyone. We were short $1200 to pay church bills. I said, "We've got to trust God." One Sunday morning, a young woman gave me an envelope. When I got home I gave it to my wife, there was $1200 in it. This lady was fighting a case of murder and she went to prison for life. She was the one who donated that money.

Extraordinary Stories of Former-Prisoners:

2. "ABC MINISTRY"

Founder, George Medley

George, 45 years old, had been incarcerated numerous times. What he has done for the community since his conversion is phenomenal. He and his wife Irene own a business called, Metal Movers. Two years ago, he started a non-profit called, ABC Ministry which supports a food pantry, a clothing bank and gives away a car every Saturday. They feed about 1,000 people a month.

This is all happening at Metal Movers, in Denver, Colorado, the business he started. His business has 45 employees and over 6 million in sales annually. He leads a weekly Bible study at his business and 22 people attend. He also started a church and on Saturdays over 100 people attend the worship service each week. George's vision for the future is to start an orphanage and to help high risk teenagers.

ABC MINISTRY is located at Metal Movers Inc., their address is: 48 East 56th Avenue, Denver, CO 80216. Website: www.metalmovers.net.

"40 Pages of My Mission Statement" by George Medley

I grew up in a predominately black neighborhood. When I was six years old, someone knocked on the door. It was Rev. Jackson and he asked my mother if he could take us children to church. My mother said it was fine. All of my siblings and myself started attending church and got saved on the altar. Even though I became a Christian, I was shop lifting and selling candy on the church bus. Once I got caught stealing crayons. My father sent me back to the store to return them.

My father was a truck driver. My parents loved us but they used alcohol and drugs. They had a bad marriage. They were always fighting and they abused us physically and verbally. I had three sisters. I was the only son. I got arrested when I was 11 or 12 years old for stealing a car. When I was in the 8th grade, I stole my dad's drugs and started selling with my friend. When my father caught me, he wanted half of the money from selling drugs so I gave him half. I stayed out of trouble for a while until I left home, I was 14 years old and in the 9th grade. I started smoking weed when I was 13 years old, using meth, cocaine, and then heroin at 16 years old. I got arrested for stealing a car when I was 15 years old.

My parents got divorced and my younger sister ended up in an orphanage. My father and I moved to Texas then he went back to my mother to reconcile. When I went to live with them, they gave me $50, told me to go back to west Texas. I stayed in town, started hanging around. I became homeless, and lived in a motel, a laundry mat, and a van. Sometimes when I was hungry, I went to a restaurant and after eating, I would run from the restaurant. I was able to work construction. As the building progressed, I was able to sleep inside the unfinished building.

I was married when I was 29 years old and my wife Irene was 25, she didn't know I was using drugs. The reason I came to Colorado was because I was a fugitive from New Mexico facing 30 years. Also, in Colorado, I was facing life in prison. I got bonded out of jail, and went on the run, ended up getting busted in Albuquerque, New Mexico.

God gave me a miracle and I didn't have to go to prison instead I became a free man. Shortly after that I went back to my old lifestyle. It didn't take long and I got real bad and went back to jail for driving with no driver's license. I served six months in Arapahoe County Jail and six months in Adams County Detention Facility.

The best thing happened while incarcerated in Arapahoe county jail. I started reflecting and counting all the faces of all the people I had conflict with 12 or 13 people over the last 24 hours. They are all punks. Then I thought to myself: "How can all those people be wrong." I didn't like what I was seeing in the mirror. A day or two later, someone asked, "Does anyone want to go to church?" Only one went, myself and the minister. The man who led the Bible study said, "Your problem is you never surrendered your life to God." That got me thinking.

I started reading the Bible and the words touched me: "Do not worry about tomorrow" and "Seek ye first God's kingdom." I questioned. How can I seek God's kingdom? I never worked for God. Then God gave me a vision like a television screen, convicting me of all the things I did wrong. I thought I needed to change. I cried out to God to forgive me. The Lord told me to lead the Bible study but I didn't know hardly anything about the Bible, still I tried to be obedient. The next thing I did was knock on all the cell doors and ask people to come out and join the Bible study. The first time, I had five or six people then it grew up to 20 people.

I was in jail but I didn't care where I was. I started serving God. That gave me a sense of purpose. I was in the elevator because Irene came to visit me. A man said, "You look happy. Are you high on something?"

I replied, "Yes, I am high on the Holy Spirit."

I made business plans so I can reach out to others. It was called ABC ministry. I wanted to create a business where I could help the poor. I didn't have to wait until I got out, the poor people were everywhere, especially in jail. I started giving away in jail with commissary by sharing with others who didn't have money. God has given me a gift of compassion, generosity and faith.

I wrote a 40 page mission statement which was a letter to Jesus. It was like, "Help me to quit talking foolishness," etc. My cellmate was 18 years old and I read the Bible to him. I stood up and read my 40 page mission statement and prayers along with Scriptures. I read it out loud everyday. Sometimes it took about two hours. That made an impact on my cell mate and me.

I started watching what I was talking since I was asking God to help me quit talking nonsense. Once I was cussing and God told me to quit cussing. So, I quit cussing but I was still cussing in my mind when I was upset. One day I had an urge to cuss in my mind and God knew it. Suddenly I realized that God didn't want me to cuss in my mind either. The Lord can read my mind and I have to clean up inside and outside. That was a new revelation to me. When nobody was looking, God was watching. Eventually I was able to stop cussing in my mind and I realized I had to control my thought life. Be careful how you think. Your life is guided by your thoughts.

I decided that I shouldn't be using drugs anymore. I was in a mental hospital twice before. I was diagnosed as bipolar, sociopathic and had been prescribed many different medications. I was using meth, cocaine, then heroin for 16 years. I didn't want to take the pills anymore. I said to myself, "You have been on street drugs all my life and you don't need any more drugs." When the medication cart showed up, I signed a refusal form. They were concerned and questioned me. Because of my explosive behavior, my nick name was "time bomb." They thought I would be like a time bomb if I don't take medication. I replied, "I want to clean up. I have been on street drugs and I don't want to do that anymore." I needed my mind renewed not meds. I was able to handle a new life with no medication. Since I started serving God, I struggled thinking I wasted all my life for Satan's kingdom. I was struggling because I thought I had to be perfect in order to serve the Lord. But I learned that it was a lie from the devil trying to make me stop serving God and to discourage me by reminding me of my past sins. One day I shared this with a man and he said, "God is not finished, he can still use you." This man's words encouraged me.

After I was released, I had to chase my old friends away to stay clean. God changed my heart and my life. I used to live in sin and I was proud of it. But I hate sin now. Before I came to know God, I didn't care about people but now I sincerely care about people. I went to the Heritage Christians Center (Potter's House now) and started to get involved in prison ministry for writing letters to prisoners. This man who encouraged me with the word that God can still use me was the first man I wrote a letter of encouragement to.

I struggled with remorse and guilt feelings. I was sorry for what I did in the past. God had forgiven me but I had a difficult time letting my past go. I felt I was not good enough to serve the Lord. I have read, *Don't Judge My Future by My Past* by Dennis Leonard. That book encourages me and I don't have to live in the past, but live in the present and focus on serving God instead of being discouraged.

I promised to God that I will donate the first $1,000 I earned, it took a while. Finally, when I had the money, I gave it to the church to help others. My finances didn't get better right away. In fact, I went through hardships but I said, "You take that devil, I am not quitting. I will keep giving. I am not giving up."

Before I finally gave myself to the Lord, I used to pray while doing dope, selling dope, and put drug money on the offering plate. I couldn't even get through the church service during the sermon. I had to go to the bathroom to snort cocaine. I couldn't wait to get through the worship service. I was selling drugs and was trying to feed the poor. This process didn't work. This time I quit smoking, drugs, alcohol, and never used again.

God is sending people to work with me in the ministry. He provides all the resources and the Lord knows I cannot do this by myself. My wife is the anchor of my life. She walks by faith. She has really been an example of the heart of God, "Mercy."

The building I operate my business in didn't come easy. My background at the time wasn't established enough to prove I was credit worthy to rent the building. When I finally meet the owners, they turned out to be Jewish. While the man was reading my application, I waited for 30 minutes. I told him that the man he was reading about in the paper was not me. I shared my testimony of how God changed my life. I had so much criminal background. I had no character references. So I asked him to call my pastor. The man called my pastor and he said, "I trust George with my building so you can trust him with your building." So, I got the building. God gave me Ephesians 3:20 and I am living it now. It says, *"Now to him who is able to do immeasurably more than all we ask or imagine, according to his power that is at work within us."*

God used Paul so God can use me. When I can I visit door to door and invite them to come to church. One day God was directing me to visit a house and they started attending our church and they brought the rest of their family. We need to develop an ear for God's voice then obey it.

I used to have a negative impact on others but now I can make a positive impact. I only have an 8th grade education, was in and out of jail, and didn't know the Lord. I used to say how I grew up in a crummy family. I cannot blame my parents. They didn't know the Lord. I used to hate them but I forgave them. I went through hell, but I realized that I needed God. "Thank you, God." I had to go through many hardships. I needed hope. I realized that I needed God. All we have to do is "surrender." God can use me to honor Him. The most important thing to me is winning souls. I used to be a hard working criminal but now I work hard for the Lord. A wise man wins souls.

Q: Any words to prisoners for encouragement?

You can use all your past mistakes and failures as stepping stones to realize that you need the Lord. Your past doesn't have to be your future. Don't waste your time on TV talk shows and playing cards. The key to having a successful life is to renew your mind with the Word of God. If you don't change your mind, you cannot change your life.

Q: Any words to families of the incarcerated?

Don't give up on them because God doesn't give up on them either. I had many people praying for me; my faithful wife Irene and my younger sister were praying for me. Many years ago, when I was visiting my sister, she said, "You are going to quit drugs and you are going to be a minister." She spoke a word of faith to me and at the time I thought she was "nuts." I didn't believe what she had said but it happened.

Q: Any words to people who struggles with addiction?

I used to pray and ask God as I was having a needle in my arm, "How long are you going to let me do this?" What I didn't realize at the time was that God is not going to do it for me. God wants us to exercise our freedom and we have to make the decision. Many times I overdosed. I finally realized that God wanted me to say "No" to temptations to alcohol and drugs. Temptation still comes but I say no to the world, sin, the devil, alcohol and drugs. Every time I said no, my faith got stronger. God honors my obedience. The Scriptures says, *"and to knowledge, self-control; and to self-control, perseverance; and to perseverance, godliness."* (2 Peter 1:6) God's Word is sowing and reaping what you sow and you will reap good or bad.

Q: What steps must a person take when they struggle with addiction?
1. Turn your life to Christ.
2. Have reverence toward God.
3. Renew your mind by reading the Bible.
4. Change your companions.
5. Act what you have learned from the Bible. What you sow is what you reap. *Mark 4:24 says, "'Consider carefully what you hear,' he continued. 'With the measure you use, it will be measured to you — and even more.'"*

Q: What are your regrets in life?
    I wasted so much time in the past and I feel badly for all the people I have hurt. God forgave me my sins and I am thankful. I regret I did not surrender sooner. I should have done this sooner.

Extraordinary Stories of a Former-Prisoner's Wife:

3. Irene Chavez

The organizer of ABC Ministry

Irene is George Medley's wife. She has never struggled with addiction of alcohol, drugs or been incarcerated. But she endured greatly when her husband, George, suffered from addiction and was in and out of jails and prisons.

I believe every successful story behind any prisoner is someone who believed in them. Some families abandon their loved ones, but some continue to believe in them and have hope that they will change someday. They support their family member no matter what happens. Many families of prisoners suffer when their family members are incarcerated. Many times they feel helpless about watching their loved ones destroy themselves by addiction or destructive behaviors. This is what Irene felt but she continued to pray for him and give him support.

The following story is from Irene, George's wife. George's successful transition in the community and leadership is the result of God's grace.

"NO REGRETS" by Irene

I am 42 years old and I grew up in a loving family. My mother, Maria, was my best friend and taught me to be a peace maker. My step dad, Peter, taught me to have respect for others. He was in the military and we traveled a lot. I had faith in God since I was little. My mother told me Jesus was real. When I had nightmares, she told me to ask Jesus for help. I had some spiritual experiences that I will never forget. There was a room in my house that I was scared to go into. One day I closed my eyes and prayed, "Jesus, I don't want to be here." Two times, when I opened my eyes, I was transported to a different level of the house. God was so real to me. I finished college with a Bachelor's degree in marketing and graphic design and became a commercial artist.

While living in Albuquerque, New Mexico, I met a man named, "David" at a party through a friend. I dated him for a couple of years. He had property and was selling cars. We got married and there were lots of things I didn't know about him. I kept my last name since I was an artist and as I look back it was a good thing since David had many secrets. He was wanted in two different states and was using different names.

The first time I found out that he was using an alias, was when my step son, Josh, came to visit, he said, "My father has two names." When my husband came home, I asked, "Do you have two names?" He denied it and said, "You know how kids make up stories." I believed him.

I had no clue that George had been on drugs for a long time. He was real good at covering up. I've never been around people who used drugs, so I was blinded to think that since he was drinking a lot, he was just sick. But his behaviors got worse and worse.

One day I was stunned when I saw stacks of money on the desk. Another time I opened the refrigerators in the garage and I was surprised to see blocks of marijuana. I saw a big car that was filled with marijuana. I know now why all the cabinets in the garage had locks. I wondered what was inside of it.

Three years after I got married, the police raided my mother's home and my husband was arrested. But this time the police told us his name was not David but George. He was in and out of jail a lot since then. I got phone calls from family members telling me George was being chased by the police and the helicopter, which was shown on the news. He was wanted by the FBI. I had no idea what was happening to him. I was getting upset, anxious, and feeling confused when local police arrested me because I was George's wife. They thought I was doing something wrong just because I was with George. I was devastated and traumatized. I was living in shock and fear. I lived as if I was holding my breath all the time.

George was constantly getting into trouble. Everything was happening so fast and I didn't know how to help him. Plus he had anger problems. One day he got into fights with 11 people either shouting back and forth or fist fighting in one hour. I tried to calm him, but I wasn't able to. He got kicked out of places because he was bullying people or he didn't like the way they looked at him. He didn't care about anything. He was drinking all the time. He didn't consider anyone else's feelings, as if he had no conscience. Later he told me he was doing heavy drugs until 2004, but all that time I thought he was just drunk. I had no idea he was doing drugs. Sometimes I smelled something but he told me it was chemicals from working on a car.

Sometimes he was up for 6 days then slept 7 days. I woke him up twice a day, gave him food and he went back to sleep. I felt he was committing suicide little by little. One day his whole body was yellow. I took him to urgent care but they were closed. I took him to a motel to take care of him. I wanted him to pass out so I could take care of him. He kept insisting that we should leave the motel.

I kept telling him I needed to go to the restroom. I remember praying, "Lord, please make him pass out so he can stay here, so he wouldn't get into trouble." I had gone to the bathroom five times. He wasn't thinking clearly, he didn't even realize that I went to the restroom so many times. He finally passed out. I took care of him. I had to sell the cars to pay the rent.

I was in turmoil when I sensed that he was using some kind of heavy drugs because of his massive mood swings. I didn't know how to help him. All I could think to do was pray. I lived like this for 12 years. We were in and out of motels, pop up camper, cooking and trying to take care of him. I thought he was sick. Nobody wants to leave when someone is sick. I thought he would die or he would kill himself by overdose or kill somebody else. It was like being in a constant state of shock.

One time I was so upset I was going to leave him. My mother said, "If you leave him in the worst time of his life, you will never forgive yourself." So, I prayed, "Lord, I will stay and help him. When he is healed, then I will leave him."

George was again arrested. When he got out of jail, I went to pick him up but I couldn't find him. Later, I learned that he walked to the bar. The police arrested him again for fighting in the bar. This happened while his son was with us. The police raided my home so many times. There were times he was arrested four times in one month.

Another time he went on a drive with our dog, Grizzley and came back without him. He didn't even realize that he took our dog. I loved Grizzley and I had to go and find him.

I've learned that a drug addict and alcoholic lies constantly. He lied about where he was. He would be gone for a little while, he was gone for two days to two weeks. I was in agony and worried about him but when he came back, I felt relieved. I never locked him out of the house, so he could always come home. I was glad he was not living in the alleys and was alive when he came back. I fixed meals for him.

When this pattern persisted, I prayed, "Lord don't let him treat me like this anymore. I hated being alone." My mother would move in many times to comfort me. He was gone so much and so many times I would get a phone call from a jail and George said, "You got to come and bail me out." He was so messed up.

One day I was crying and praying. Then I felt someone was in the room and I saw a big face in the room, a part of eyes and nose. I believe God literally appeared to me to comfort me. After that I didn't feel alone any more.

George's sister gave me advice. She said, "You have to claim things." I started praying. "Lord, this is beneficial for you, for George and me. Thank you for making George just like you, Jesus." At that time I didn't believe it and I was crying, but I kept repeating it out loud. Faith comes by healing but at the same time I could hear a negative voice, "That's the biggest lie you are saying." Then I would say it out loud, "Thank you for making George like you." I kept proclaiming it. I didn't see the vision for the future but my sister-in-law's words encouraged me.

I read Scriptures to George, prayed for him, and played Christian music when he was in the car. He hated it and turned it off. I would lay my hand over his head when he was sleeping and prayed over him without touching his head. I kept praying for his healing.

We lived in Colorado about nine years. Every time I was at the breaking point and couldn't handle it or breathe, he went to jail. That was a break for me as if God knew I needed a break.

At that time I felt so exhausted. I weighted 98 pounds with all the worries and stress I had to endure until I was 36 years old. All the police raids and I was worrying that he was driving. He didn't have a driver's license plus he was always arguing, and obnoxious. He was not in his right mind. He would wake me up when I slept, just to tell me to scoot over. During twelve years of panic every day was the same, passing my birthday, never celebrated an anniversary.

In 2005 the last time he went to jail, I went to visit him. And it was the first time he asked me, "How are you doing?" This was the first time I noticed that he was changed. After he was released, he said he was saving $1,000 to give to God and he did. He said he was going to serve God. I didn't believe it at first because he had lied to me so many times. He didn't like the way he was living and wanted to change. So, I thought to myself I will give him six months to make sure he had changed, to make sure he was going to be okay and live.

I waited a few months and one day he said, "I am going to go to the store and I will be back." Anytime he said that to me before, he lied to me and went to find drugs. This time he didn't disappear. I was finally convinced that he was healed. He started watching praise and worship service on TV and reading the Bible. I was so drained at that point though. I was grateful to God that George was not going to die.

George said, "I can take care of things now."

I said, "You never apologized for how you treated me for all these years."

He said, "Well, I'm sorry."

I said, "That doesn't cut it."

George asked, "Don't you love me any more?"

"After all these years I find it hard to like you but I don't want you to die."

He said he could handle everything. I felt like my job was finished. I don't have to be around him anymore since I told the Lord when he was healed, I would leave him. Just before I walked out, I knew in my mind, I was never coming back. I was comforted by that thought.

When I was in the truck, and I heard a man's voice twice telling me, "George is not your enemy." I knew that came from the Lord. All of a sudden I had a revelation. George isn't my enemy. The devil was the enemy. George was used by the devil for so long. The Lord had to speak to me to change my mind.

I went back inside and I told him about the voice I heard and said, "Everything is going to be alright."

It took almost a year until I could finally believe that he was a changed man. But for so long, I suffered from bad memories and I had to change my way of thinking as well. When he was doing drugs, he would talk softly. After George changed, he talked softly. That reminded me of when he was on drugs. I was on alert all the time to discern if what he was doing was truly changed behavior or not.

I learned to say, "Satan get behind me. He is a changed man of God."

After that I was able to trust him. I had to tell myself literally. I need to submit to him. That is the hardest thing that I ever had to learn. I had to heal from fear and relearn how to live.

Still, if someone would have told me about what we would be doing for the Lord in later years, I would have never believed it. God was merciful to me. He helped me to forgive and have compassion for my husband.

My name, "Irene" means peaceful. It seems as though God surrounded me with a protective bubble. He gave me the wisdom to know that George was sick. I learned not to get angry with little things. You learn to pick your battles. No one is going to be loving all the time. God gives us examples of love in the Scripture: *"Love is patient, love is kind. It does not envy, it does not boast, it is not proud. It is not rude, it is not self-seeking, it is not easily angered, it keeps no record of wrongs. Love does not delight in evil but rejoices with the truth. It always protects, always trusts, always hopes, always perseveres. Love never fails."* (1 Corinthians 13:4-8a)

God loved George and showed His love through me. The Lord also gave me the ability to endure. George didn't like people and couldn't stand being around them. Now he loves people. Only God can do that, change a man's heart. He went from a hater of people to a lover of people.

Q: Any words to prisoners for encouragement?

This is the shortest time we have compared to eternity. This life is where we prove ourselves. Do we want to honor God for eternity or are we too stubborn to do things His way? Our enemy tries to force us to look down and that is a waste of time. I pray, "I am not only grateful that you love us, but that you made yourself known to us. You could have existed and not even made yourself known."

Q: Any words to families of the incarcerated?

You cannot blame someone who doesn't know better. You cannot blame a man who is blind that they cannot see. That may be your incarcerated family member's case. Continue praying for them and stand in the gap – constant prayer, and encouragement to the prisoners will help them. Rely on God, so you can get through it with His help. God helped me to get through it. Remember that no matter how bad I thought I had been treated or how rough it had been for me, I always knew George had it worse. He hated himself and hated his life. So, have mercy on your family member who struggles from addiction.

Q: Any words to people who struggle with addiction?

Hold every thought captive and compare it to the will of God. The only way of knowing that is to know the Bible.

Read the Word that is alive and talk to God. George never stumbled after God changed him, and I am talking about someone who loved sin, but he never went back to his old ways.

Q: What steps must a person take when they struggle with addiction?
1. Submit to God.
2. Repent.
3. Devote time to Him, read the Bible, talk to him, wait on Him, wait for an answer.
4. Change your circle of influences, friends, and find a church where you can grow spiritually.
5. Don't go back to your familiar environment but focus on Jesus.

Q: Any miracles that you have experienced that you cannot forget?

George is a miracle to me. He had no conscience and cared about nothing but now he cares about everything. He cares about God more than anything, and he cares about God's people. George is a man after God's heart. He is not ashamed of the gospel. If someone is upset while waiting in the grocery line, he will talk to others about God while waiting. His whole life is focused on spreading the gospel of Jesus. Without the Lord, he told me he didn't have a reason to get out of the bed. His purpose has to be living for the Lord and George is living it now.

Q: What are your regrets in life?

If I changed anything, the outcome would be different. I don't know if I would change anything. George and I both needed to grow. I was really naive and I had to be strong for my husband. I am amazed with what God has done with us, serving God together. George is a servant of God and I stand by him. I couldn't have asked for anything more. If you asked me that question ten years ago, I would have had a lot of answers for you. Lots of regrets at the time but God didn't show me the end result. If He had, I would have had more hope, then it really wouldn't be a true molding of my character. God doesn't give us the whole picture of our lives.

Q: How are you involved in ministry?

George is the visionary and he sees the finished products. He gives me directions on what I should do to help him to accomplish it. I organize the food bank. I purchase food and oversee what needs to be done to make things go smooth. We have many volunteers: my Aunt Julia, Arlene and about five others including a USF Trucking Company which picks up the food and delivers for us. When people donate cars, the profit goes to the food bank. We are serving about 1,000 people every month. We give two big bags of groceries to each person who comes to the food bank.

Extraordinary Stories of Former Prisoners:

4. "OPEN DOOR, YOUTH GANG ALTERNATIVES"

Founder Rev. Leon Kelly

Reverend Leon Kelly is 58 years young and serves as the Executive Director of Open Door Youth Gang Alternatives. He is the founder and driving force behind this ministry. Open Door is the oldest anti-gang program still in existence in the Denver metro area, a one-of-a-kind agency that was founded in December, 1987. It is a non-profit, non-law enforcement agency with the sole mission of curbing gang recruitment, and reducing street gang violence. Open Door Youth Gang Alternatives reaches kids through a variety of activities that include in-school and after-school programs, parenting classes, employment and job training for teens, family and victim support, gang mediation and intervention, public education and community awareness. Rev. Kelly began his ministry 28 years ago when he noticed changes occurring within Denver including a huge influx of gangs from California. He experienced difficult times as a young man himself. He served three years in a Colorado penitentiary on a 5-8 year sentence.

One of the components of his ministry is an after-school program in one of Denver's schools. The after-school program serves approximately 180-200 children ages 6-14. It provides academic support as well as character education with a strong emphasis on self-discipline and self-improvement, all in an effort to help the children make positive choices when confronted by negative influences.

Rev. Kelly's work is crucial because America has the largest prison population in the world. Many children are growing up without parents, especially fathers. Many children who joined gangs had moms who cared for them but most of them grew up without a dad figure in their lives.

Without a dad figure in a child's life, there is something missing—security and protection and nurturing etc. Unless someone can fill that gap, these children may be searching for a father figure in the wrong place like in the streets and through gang affiliation. That's what Rev. Kelly tries to prevent. He became a father to many children. He is trying to save children from gangs, prison, and early violent death.

When Rev. Kelly saw the need, he acted on it. Open Door Youth Gang Alternatives has been reaching out to many who choose to walk the right path. He is educating the public and children about the dangers of being involved in gangs and how to avoid the destructive path of addiction, gangs, and prison. He continues to be a positive role model for many people in the community and brings transformation to many by reaching out to young children.

In Rev. Kelly's office, he has a list of the young people who have died a violent death in the Denver metro area. As of June 18, 2011, there had been 996 since he started ministry. Many of them he knew. One of the records Rev. Kelly holds is that he has buried more young people in the State than any other minister, sometimes burying two or three young people in a week. It is not a record that he is proud of, but through these deaths he has had the privilege of supporting the families as they go through these difficult times. The list on the wall reminds him that there is still plenty of work to do. It motivates him to continue his work.

In 2010, Rev. Kelly received a pardon from the Colorado Governor. His tireless work for kids and the community have been recognized by many people and organizations. Receiving a pardon was something that Rev. Kelly is proud of. He certainly deserves it. We don't have any idea how many children are saved from dying violent deaths and gang related criminal activities because of his efforts. I believe there will be many more people who are touched by his ministry.

OPEN DOOR YOUTH GANG ALTERNATIVES is located at 1615 California #712, Denver, Colorado, 80202, 303-893-gang (4264). Website: www.therev.org. Open Door is a non-profit, community based, non-law enforcement organization.

"MY STORY" by Rev. Leon Kelly

I am a PK (preacher's kid); my grandfather and father were ministers. My mother was a preacher's wife and missionary, and she had the highest position in the church as a woman. My parents had six children, three sons and three daughters. I am the first born male and my dad taught me about hard work and instilled the importance of a strong work ethic in my life. My father was a pillar in the community. I didn't want to be a pastor because of what I saw him go through. Although I was not interested in ministry, I still attended church three or four times a week and all day on Sunday. Faith and my relationship with God was always a big part of my life. I played basketball and football at East High School in Denver and headed to University of Colorado (CU) for college.

When I left home and started attending CU in Boulder, I was exposed to a new world. The hedge that had been built around me was no longer there. I had no protection and college life was a life of temptation. I was a star athlete being placed on a pedestal. I was 18 years old. I was invited to parties. I started drinking, using drugs. And along with that came the females and my first introduction to greed. Eventually, I gave in and started selling drugs. I was still able to continue my studies somehow, and graduated in 1975.

After returning to Denver, I played semi-professional basketball. I was doing well. Yet, I continued to sell and use cocaine and other drugs, a secret my family knew nothing about.

One day I was standing on my balcony in my downtown penthouse and thought, "There has to be something more to life than this. I know better than this." I struggled as soon as I started thinking about it, then I was right back to selling and using drugs. At times I thought I was on top of the world, and then down I went. I had an experience that caused me to reflect on my life. I found myself in a situation that goes along with the game. I thought I had shot someone in the head. When I turned around, the man's forehead had a crease — blood was gushing out. Although I had only grazed his head, fear came over me and I realized that I could have killed him.

As time went on, my dark side eventually caught up with me. I was arrested. My family bailed me out of jail. After going through the criminal process I was convicted. Upon going to court for sentencing the judge said he saw something in me that he normally didn't see in his courtroom. A young man with a college degree and a supporting cast of family and friends. I thought I was going to get probation, yet he sentenced me to 5-8 years. It was like the bubble had popped. I was going to prison and I was a preacher's kid. They handcuffed me and all my family couldn't believe it. I was transported from Denver County Jail to prison in Canon City, Colorado. The images I thought about prison were what I saw on TV. I couldn't believe it. I had a college degree and was playing basketball and I was going to jail.

After arriving at Territorial Prison, my reputation as a ball player and dope man came to light and other inmates wanted to be around me. The reality set in and I asked myself, "How can I adapt to this environment?" I began selling drugs and running a store out of my cell. I, basically, continued my negative lifestyle behind bars.

My parents visited me in prison. I never saw my mother cry before, but she cried. It pricked my spirit and I said, "Mom I am sorry." My mom said, "How can you say sorry after sending us all through this?????" I replied, "Mom I am going to change but I really don't know how." She said, "Talk to God just like you talk to me." I battled with the conflict of how could I sell drugs and still call myself a Christian. While in prison I saw horrible things. A man was raped and killed and that impacted me greatly. It still haunts me now. Another guy was stabbed and the blood gushed out of him. What could I have done to save these men? I am still hurting for them. I went back to my cell and prayed that God would work in me. I was remembering my mother's words. As I continued to pray it was as if a weight was lifted off of me. For me, mom's suggestion worked. It doesn't matter where you are. If you are sincere about it, you can do it. All of this led me to stop selling and I started leading Bible studies. Four people grew into forty. When the other inmates saw that I was sincere, it became a way of life. God was preparing me for his work.

I started taking a Bible study correspondence course to learn more about the Word of God. I asked myself "Who am I and what powers do I have." One Saturday I was called to the control center and was told to pack it up, "You are out of here." No one knew I was being released. When I showed up at home my family was so surprised, maybe they thought I had escaped. When I told them I was paroled early, they were overjoyed.

I still had one package of cocaine stashed that I had kept to use when I got out to help me get back on my feet. As I retrieved the package, I thought about all the good times with drugs, but I knew I had to let it go. I opened the package and spread it on the ground and I said, "Satan I rebuke you in the name of Jesus, you have no more power over me." That was the last turning point in my life. I finally realized who I was. It all became very real to me.

There were many challenges I had to deal with now, being an ex-convict. Although I had always interviewed well, having a record changed everything. Potential employers never called back. I remember feeling the urge to give up, but something inside of me challenged me to continue. I went to another interview and I told myself that I have to do something different. I spoke candidly with the interviewer and told him, "I know my worth; my challenge is to prove to you what I am capable of. I will work for you for two weeks for free to prove to you that I would be an asset to your company. There would be nothing for you to lose." It was a recycling company. The company agreed to try me out. I was told to be there at 8:00 a.m. and I arrived every day at 7:30 a.m. I was the first one to arrive and the last one to leave. At the end of the first week, the supervisor said, "Kelly, I want to see you. The first thought that came to my mind was that he was going to have to let me go since I wasn't being paid and it would be against company policy. But, he told me that he had noticed my work ethic and he thought I would be a valuable employee. I had proved my worth. He put me on the schedule for the following week and agreed to pay me for the week as well. Within one month, I became a supervisor.

In 1984, gangs really started migrating to Denver from California. Crips came to the east side of the city and Bloods claimed Park Hill, a neighborhood east of downtown. At the time I had become the athletic director at a local gym. I was able to establish relationships with the youth in the east side neighborhood including many gang members. When I started to experience firsthand the LA influence, I knew that in order to deal with this negative mind-set, I had to learn more. I went to Los Angeles, California to find out firsthand what Denver was in for. Upon returning to Denver, I attempted to warn the city fathers including the mayor and city council members in an effort to be pro-active. Their response about this potential plague was that they didn't want to cause panic. They wanted to take time to evaluate and analyze just how serious this problem was becoming. In the mean time, it continued to spread. The shootings in the beginning were meant to only intimidate. They now were hitting their marks, and kids were dying left and right. Over time, the police and elected officials realized that we had a bigger problem on our hands than they originally thought. They needed me, just as much as the kids that were dying on the streets did. I finally realized that I was doing what God had prepared me to do.

Q: Any words to prisoners for encouragement?
They have to be true to what God has done for them. Understand who they are in Christ and then be consistent when they get out. Challenges will come and they must be prepared for them.

Q: Any words to families of the incarcerated?
God has a way of putting out a stumbling block to get our attention and sometimes being locked up could be a blessing in disguise. If I hadn't been incarcerated, my life wouldn't have been changed so dramatically. I could have been killed or worse taken another's life. It gave me a wake-

up call. Encourage your sons or daughters to ask themselves, what am I supposed to learn from this? What is God saying to me? What's the message you want to give me?

Q: Any words to a person who struggles with addiction?
Addiction has no respect for people. I was blessed that I didn't have to go through a physical rehab even though at times, I was doing $600 a day of drugs. But, for some users they need that kind of support. I did go through withdrawal and it affected me emotionally and physically, but again, I felt as though this was all part of my "Godly" training. So, ask yourself, "What is the purpose of changing?" This question is important for those who want to change.

Q: What steps must a person take when they struggle with addiction?
Be true to yourself. Accept that you have a problem. Let go of your blame and take responsibility. Have faith in the lord but understand that even though you may have all the faith in the world, without works, it is dead.

Q: Any miracles that you have experienced that you will never forget?
The first one that comes to my mind was when I was in my early 30's, and it was a Memorial Day weekend — I began hemorrhaging and spitting up blood. I ended up in the intensive care unit. I spent six days and after hearing the men of medicine say that they had done all that they could do, I thought, "What is going on?" God came to me and said, "I still have work for you to do." I realized that all of us are mortal. We all have a purpose. God had spared me again and had allowed me to continue my work of trying to save others.

Q: What are your regrets in life?

First of all, I regret disappointing my mom and dad with some of the decisions and actions that I made before going to prison. I realize that they forgave me a long time ago and through my good works I have been able to save many. It's still hard for a son, to remember the pain in his parent's eyes and know that he was responsible.

Secondly, I still struggle with forgiving myself. I realize that if I hadn't had the journey that I did, I wouldn't be the man I am today. A pastor reminded me that God forgives us before we are even born. And, the State forgave me in 2010 when the governor granted me an official pardon. Yet, I still regret the lives that I touched negatively. I always say that I don't condone the negative actions of some of the youth I deal with, but I value their lives. Above all, I have learned how precious and yet, fleeting life is.

Chapter 4

Reflections
by
Yong Hui McDonald

1. The Man's Tears

I once met an inmate, a big man in his mid 30's, weeping day and night. A deputy asked me to see him. When I asked him what was troubling him, he told me that the day of his release was approaching and he didn't have any place to go.

I gave him names of some homeless shelters, but we both had no assurance that he would be admitted – there aren't very many places for homeless people. Before his incarceration he was homeless and he was afraid of going back out on the street. This big man couldn't stop crying. I felt so bad that Adams County didn't have a homeless shelter. Other counties don't have enough homeless shelters either.

When I was working as a volunteer at Samaritan House, a homeless shelter in Denver, Colorado, they didn't have enough room either. They can only house a limited amount of people. Then every night, they will let 100 people in to sleep on the floor on a mattress. After one hundred people, they couldn't let any more people in and many are still standing in the line.

I learned that many inmates who don't have places to go end up coming back to the facility. For homeless people, jail and prison is a safe place. It's a real sad story.

2. Why Lord?

I didn't understand how underprivileged the mentally ill are until I started working in prisons and jails.

One day, during my school years, I was leading worship at San Carlos Correctional Facility in Pueblo where there are many mentally ill inmates. I led three worship services for small groups of people.

During one of these services God spoke to my heart. He said, "I have these people here for their protection." I couldn't believe it. I had heard of the violence in jails and prisons. "Why? Why, God? How could prison be safer than home for some people?" I couldn't help but cry.

When I was working at DWCF, I was visiting the maximum security unit one day. In one room, I saw the floor was flooded and a woman in the room kept flushing the toilet. I was told that she thought she could take a shower if she kept flushing it.

In the maximum unit they can come out of the room one hour a day, walk around the narrow hallway, talk to other maximum inmates and also take a shower. I learned that many inmates do not belong in jail but they need special care, maybe a mental hospital.

3. God Was There

One day a man in medical wanted to have a Bible. When I met this young man in his early 20's, he was upset that the Bible he received had the ACDF stamp on it. He said, "To me this is like the anti-Christ's stamp."

I replied, "No, that doesn't have anything to do with anti-Christ. All the Bibles have a stamp on it because the Bible is the property of the facility."

This man couldn't understand why. After I heard from a deputy that this man had a brain injury, I went to the library and found a Bible with no stamp on it to make him happy and to help him let go of his frustration.

After this man received a Bible, he didn't show any emotion. I asked the man to sign his request form but he wouldn't. He just stood there and acted like he couldn't understand what I was saying.

His roommate saw what was happening. He was a very kind man. He gently explained to the young man that he needs to sign the paper. But this young man wouldn't as if he couldn't process what was happening. At that moment, I felt God's presence in that room so strong. God was there to let me know He cares about this young man. God watched what we tried to do to help the man.

I left the room and I was grieving. I thought he didn't belong in jail. He belongs in a mental hospital.

4. Crystal

I met Crystal, a beautiful young woman, 21 years old. I first met her when I was leading a prayer meeting in a pod. Crystal told me that she had no interest in God when she arrived at ACDF. Then one thing led to another, she found the Lord and her life was changed for the better. She said she was much happier because she found God.

The last day Crystal attended a chaplain's worship service, I baptized her. The whole time she was in worship, she was crying. She told me that she would be released the next day, and asked me if I knew any homeless shelters that I could refer her to. I asked her if she had the resource packet and she said yes. I told her I had no place to refer her to because there was no place that I know of that could house her.

With all the services I had led, I've never flooded with tears like that worship. I was so overwhelmed with such grief and sadness. Where can she go? What were her options? Who could help her? I was asking God to help her, but I had no way to help her. It was almost like I was telling her to go in peace but I wasn't able to help her to keep that peace. She needed a transitional home where caring people could mentor, guide, and support her until she could learn to be sufficient enough to take care of her own needs.

There was no one who could help her and that made me cry. I knew too well the resource packet she had was just addresses and numbers with no assurance whatsoever.

Crystal's story continues because there are many like her at ACDF, walking out of jail with nowhere to go. I continue to pray that God will raise someone who has a vision to help someone like Crystal, soon. Adams County should be able to care for Adams County homeless people. We need someone who understands the pain and suffering of homeless people, and can plant the seed of compassion, so many could see the fruit. I believe it could happen and will happen, someday, if we keep trying to get the ground ready and plant the seed.

5. Transformation

One day my heart was so heavy for the homeless people who will be released from the facility, but had no place to go. So, I attended an Adams County resource meeting to address this problem in hopes that someone would start a homeless shelter in Adams County. After I made an announcement, a man came up to me and introduced himself and thanked me for what I was doing. The following letter was sent to me not long after that. I have decided to share it with others because this letter encouraged me more than any of the other stories I have heard since I started working as a chaplain at ACDF.

Rev. McDonald,

I met you in the ACDF. I attended the services you offered. I know you see so many inmates you can't keep track of them but I was touched by God in there. I was looking at 36 years in prison for a fight that I got in with two other guys. Well it didn't look good for me because I thought I was going to go to prison for the rest of my life. I knew I probably deserved it because of the way I had lived my life. I was a gang member and a drug dealer for most of my life.

I did a lot of things I'm not proud of. So, when I prayed in there to give my life to God, I never expected God to change my life like He did. I got out of jail on a $20,000 bond and from there I went to a group home for men. It was like a boot camp but I made it through.

Then when I went to trial all the charges were dropped. Thank God for that and now I'm working with school district 50 and started a non-profit program called 180 Degree Gang Alternatives. For the last two years, I've been helping kids get out of gangs and helping ex-offenders find jobs, housing, and other resources.

When I saw you walk into the resource meeting, it was so awesome to see you. I just wanted to say thank you for all you do and I hope to someday be able to visit the jail and give my testimony. I am working on becoming a minister because it is all because of God that I am where I am.

For inmates, their true testing comes when they are released from jail or prison. Incarceration shelters them from many temptations from falling into alcohol, drugs and a destructive path. If one is not determined to change their life, people could go back to the old lifestyle. This man's determination to serve the Lord is truly a blessing, not only himself but to many others. His story also gives hope of what God can do when a person has faith and willingness to follow their calling. This man made it outside and is serving the Lord. That is really encouraging to me.

6. Make No Little Plans

The following sermon was published in the book, *Maximum Saints Make No Little Plans*.

"Make No Little Plans"

After World War I, Chicago Temple, the First United Methodist Church in downtown Chicago, reached a critical point. People were moving out of the downtown area, and the church's membership was shrinking. Some members thought that they should sell the church building and move to the suburbs, but this church had visionary leaders who inspired the congregation to envision a bigger sanctuary that would seat one thousand people and a twenty-six-story high building with beautiful architecture that would prepare the church for the future.

The architect, Daniel Burnham, made a famous speech: "<u>Make no little plans....make big plans; aim high in hope and work</u>....Let your church be order and your beacon beauty....think big." His vision for the church project was approved, and the new church building was dedicated on Easter morning in 1952. Each year, thousands of people make a pilgrimage to visit Chicago Temple. I had the privilege of visiting this church and was inspired by the beautiful architecture of the sanctuary, and the building.

This church is growing in membership, and also in ministry opportunities, because over the period of time since the new church was built, big apartment complexes have been built, and the population grew. Also, this church developed mission programs to feed the poor and homeless, and developed art ministry. All of this was possible because they made big plans.

This story teaches us a great spiritual lesson. We have to be visionaries if we want to serve the Lord. We need to make big plans to serve His kingdom. Unless we plan it, we are not going to see the result. He made big plans to save us through Jesus. *"God so loved the world that He gave His one and only Son, that whoever believes in Him shall not perish but have eternal life."* (John 3:16)

Jesus also told us to make big plans to save people. He said, *"Therefore go and make disciples of all nations, baptizing them in the name of the Father and of the Son and of the Holy Spirit, and teaching them to obey everything I have commanded you. And surely I am with you always, to the very end of the age."* (Matthew 28:19-20) Jesus believes that we have great potential and can make a difference in the world. He said, *"I tell you the truth, anyone who has faith in me will do what I have been doing. He will do even greater things than these, because I am going to the Father."* (John 14:12)

Jesus has the power to help us. He pulls us out of the pit if we ask Him for help. Jesus has faith in us, even when we make mistakes. When we ask Jesus for forgiveness, He forgives us. He brings healing when we are wounded and hurting. He carries us when we don't have the strength to walk. He gives us directions as to how we can serve Him by serving others by the power of the Holy Spirit. He gives us the power to resist the devil.

The sad thing is that many Christians make little plans, even though we say that we want to serve the Lord. Many of us are making plans that are too little and we are only thinking about our own comfort. We need to stretch our minds in accordance with God's will. Jesus' plan should come first before anything else. If your plan for the future is only taking care of yourself and your family and is focused only on your financial security, you have made little plans.

I want to give you a few suggestions: For those of you who have not accepted Jesus as your personal Savior, make big plans for your eternity to be with the Lord by giving your life to Christ. You will make the best investment for your soul when you recognize that God can forgive you and save you. Here is a prayer that you can pray to accept Jesus. "Lord Jesus, I confess that I am a sinner. I believe you died on the cross for my sins and you have risen from the dead. I need your forgiveness. Please come into my heart and my life. Forgive all of my sins. Bless me with the Holy Spirit. Fill my empty heart with your love. Help me to understand your love. Bless me with the wisdom to understand I can serve you. I pray this in Jesus' name. Amen."

For those of you who are Christians but are only making little plans, start asking God to give you visions and dreams of how you can make plans to serve God to the maximum.

Remember, the Lord's big plans always move us beyond our comfort zones. His big plans always include that we hear, see, understand and feel the pain and suffering of others, and do something about it. Moses had a little plan when the Lord called him because he thought about his own comfort. He tried to give God excuses why he wouldn't be the right person. But when he obeyed the Lord, he was able to free the Israelites from slavery.

I believe Jesus has big plans for all of us because He can do much more than we can think or imagine when we obey Him. We all have goodness in us because we are created in the image of God. His creativity and many other holy characteristics are part of our nature. If you see only bad in yourself and others, you have not seen all of what God has created. Until can exercise divine characteristics and practice our goodness by loving God and loving our neighbors, we cannot be happy or feel fulfilled. Deepest joy and fulfillment can come only when we love God and our neighbors.

What about us? Do we have faith in us as much as Jesus has faith in us? Do we believe that we can make a difference in this world? Don't tell me that you don't have any special gifts. When we look into what we have, we can see that we have received many gifts. The most important gift each one of us has been given is our very life.

Unfortunately, many people do not take care of God's gift of life. They misuse their bodies and do destructive things to themselves and others. Yet, our creativity and our compassion are gifts from the Lord. Our desires to be good and to do good, are God given characteristics and are gifts. Also, our faith is a gift from God to be shared with others, and this takes planning and commitment. Your encouraging words of faith can be life saving gifts to those who do not know Christ and to those who want to grow in Christ.

Make big plans, and ask the Lord to give you directions for reaching your goal. Then be ready because the devil will try to convince you that working for God is too difficult for you or that you don't have the gifts to do it. The devil will try to convince you that you are not good enough to serve the Lord. Don't listen to the devil's lies. If you do, you will end up making little plans and grieving the Lord.

To make big plans, start with what you have. Ask the Lord how you can serve Him to the maximum with what you have. One way of examining your heart to see whether you have a big plan or a little plan, is to see if you have the passion to save the lost. If you don't feel the burden for the lost, you are making little plans.

Another way of examining your heart is to see if your plan is easily achievable. If it is, then probably your plan is too little. Every big plan for the kingdom of God stretches our imagination and goes beyond our limited thinking. Sometimes it looks impossible to reach the goal.

Also, if you make plans without being willing to pay the price, you are actually making little plans. Jesus said we cannot be His disciples unless we deny ourselves, pick up our cross and follow him. The price you have to pay is this: You have to discard your own plans and make Jesus' plan your first priority.

Sometimes, even when we think we have made big plans to serve, we still come up short. I am learning that through the book project, *Maximum Saints*. By the end of February 2006, with the help of many churches and friends, I was able to raise enough funds to order 1,500 copies of *Maximum Saints Never Hide in the Dark*. At the time, ACDF had about 1,300 inmates. I knew 1,500 copies would be enough for our facility. God spoke to me that my vision was too small. So, I ordered 10,000 copies of the book and God provided all the funds through generous people.

Make big plans to serve the Lord. That's the only way you can find happiness in this life. Even though you might be going through the fires of testing, if you make big plans to help others, you will come out with joy. If you don't make big plans, you will find that there is a big, empty hole in your heart that nothing can fill. This is one way the Holy Spirit communicates with us. When you have a restless heart, you need to learn to listen to the Lord so you can make big plans.

If you know that something is missing in your life even after you have become a Christian, it's about time that you think about making big plans to serve God. If you don't make big plans, the price you will be paying will be great. It might be that you live in misery and depression because you are only looking into your own pain, and as much as you dwell in your own pain and suffering, your wounds will grow, and it will overwhelm you. When you start looking into others' pain and start helping them, your wounds will heal.

For those of you who are incarcerated and anxious to go home, I want you to examine your heart to see what you are planning to do when you get out. If you are making little plans to serve yourself by getting drunk and using drugs, the results are always the same. You will end up living in turmoil, and there is a chance that you will be coming back to the facility for more "training."

If you make big plans to serve God and are committed to follow your plans no matter what happens, it will happen for you. If you make big plans, are you willing to pay the price to follow your calling and use your gifts to the maximum, no matter where you are? The price you have to pay is to put God's kingdom first, above everything else.

It's time that you realize that little plans cannot help build God's kingdom, but bring only misery and discontent. You will get hurt when you make little plans to serve only yourself. Whatever the price you pay to obey the Lord will be worth it because the Holy Spirit will be blessing you with joy and peace. You can also see your incarceration as God's call to mission work to save people from going to hell. Be persistent. Big plans have to be accompanied by preparation. Work toward your goal every day, moment by moment. They have to be carefully planned and need our total commitment and dedication to follow the Holy Spirit's leading. Let me leave you with a couple of questions: How many people are you planning to lead to the Lord in your lifetime? If you come up with a number, how are you planning to achieve that goal? May God bless you in your making of big plans to serve the Lord and others.

7. Revival

One of the happiest moments at ACDF is to learn of the transformation of inmates and revival, this I experience everyday. Why is it so important for me to see revival in inmates' lives? There is a reason for it.

I grew up in Korea and have seen revival. After I came to the United States in 1979, I was missing something and I knew what it was – revival. My definition of having a revival is to see: (1) Many people being saved. (2) Many lives being transformed by God's love and power. (3) Many people give their lives to serve God. (4) Many have the passion to save the lost.

If someone would have asked me what I wanted to see in America, it would be a revival. For a long time, I attended many different churches and retreats in search of God, hoping to experience a revival. Many times I sat and cried inside worship services and retreats because I couldn't feel the presence of the Lord. I asked, "Who has a passion for lost souls? Will I ever be able to see a revival? God, where are you?" I kept asking these questions, but I received no answer.

I desperately wanted to see a revival, but I was only searching for it in other people. I was a luke-warm Christian and only following worldly desires and passion. Therefore, when God called me to the ministry, I resisted. I had no desire to be a minister. Then the Lord directed me to spend time in prayer, so I started praying for a revival in America.

Soon, the Lord pointed out that the revival had to start in my heart first. While I was writing the book, *Journey With Jesus*, He convinced me of the power of the Holy Spirit. That was the turning point in my life. I finally gave up my plans, and made the decision to go into the ministry to serve Jesus. This was the beginning of my own revival.

After I started working as a chaplain at ACDF I learned that God could do much more than I could think, or imagine, if only I would follow the Holy Spirit's leading. God planted the seed of revival in my heart, and I couldn't give up the vision of seeing a revival. For a long time I lamented over the fact that I didn't see revival taking place, and thought I would never see it.

Interestingly, I have learned that many inmates at

ACDF also were praying for a revival. I believe persistent prayer is the foundation of revival. So, I started a seven-week prayer project, with different themes, to promote revival. The first prayer project I started in 2004 was praying for "Revival and Healing of Our Souls." I encouraged the inmate leaders to remind others to pray for revival in their own pods.

By the end of 2006, I had led seven different prayer projects to promote revival. During that time, I started seeing something that I had never expected—a glimpse of a revival. The Holy Spirit's presence in our facility was so powerful that we had many conversions and baptisms. Many inmates were responding to the call to serve the Lord. Within the first two years I was leading chaplain's worship services, more than 500 people had been baptized.

The Holy Spirit touched so many people who came to worship services. One day I saw that many words in the hymns were hard to read and I thought it was caused by the water from many baptisms. I asked the Chaplain's assistant if that was the reason and he told me no. "It was the tears of the inmates," he said. "I have to wipe them off after the worship services."

Then I realized the Holy Spirit had started healing many inmates' hearts. Tears bring healing. When the Lord speaks to our hearts and give us understanding we cannot help but to let the tears come. When the Holy Spirit is present, many times tears come.

At the beginning of January of 2007, the Lord asked me to go back to my first seven-week prayer project again so that inmates would pray for a revival so I did. By then, I developed "Jericho Prayer Walk," and "A Holy Fasting Prayer" and about ten prayer project brochures to help those who wanted to grow in faith and experience revival.

Until that time, I had seen the Holy Spirit's mighty power transform many lives, but I still felt I was only seeing a glimpse of the revival. Then, in the middle of the prayer project in February of 2007, for the first time, God told me that I was in the midst of the revival. I couldn't believe it, but it was true!

I believe the prayers of many people for revival were seeing the fruits of their spiritual labor. The Lord gave me understanding that the book, *Maximum Saints*, was contributing to this revival. Whenever I work on *Maximum Saints* books I have an overwhelming sense of joy. At times I am so filled with the Holy Spirit's joy, I have to say, "Calm me down Lord. I am just too excited. Calm me down." What I couldn't find outside, I found inside jail. I am so grateful that God granted me to see what I had wanted to see so badly in America—a revival through inmate leaders and their stories of the *Maximum Saints* books. Praise God!

8. One Million Dream Project

God keeps enlarging the TPPM vision. Chaplain Stanley Harrell, from the Georgia Correctional Facility, told me how much prisoners are touched by TPPM books. He asked me to send a truckload of TPPM books to the Georgia prisons because 50,000 people are incarcerated there. In 2010, TPPM sent books to the Georgia prisons, about three truck loads. Also, chaplains from other facilities mentioned that they could use more TPPM books. To respond to the growing need for these books, in 2010, TPPM started the "One Million Dream Project." The goal is to raise enough funds to distribute one million copies of each book TPPM produced. Please pray that this project will glorify the Lord and help many prisoners and homeless people who are in need of salvation, encouragement and spiritual growth.

I have many amazing stories of how God provides for this project, but I will share one of the stories of how He is enlarging our vision. While TPPM was at the final stage of editing of the book, *Maximum Saints Forgive*, God told me to visit New Gate Church in Aurora, Colorado, on August 29, 2010.

New Gate is a Korean-American congregation that supports TPPM by sending a monthly contribution. While I was driving to the church God challenged me to order 20,000 copies of *Maximum Saints Forgive*, instead of 10,000.

To order 10,000 copies, we need $5,000, but for 20,000 copies we need $8,000. When I arrived at the church, I shared this with Rev. Guan In Suk, and she asked me to announce it during the worship services. The next day, New Gate Church delivered me a check for $3,160. Because of their generous contribution, TPPM is able to order 10,000 more copies than we had planned. I was told that one person from the congregation donated $3,000 for this project. Praise the Lord! That was a miracle from God. I felt so blessed because of their concern for prisoners and homeless people.

Another vision God has given me is to reach out to more people with *Maximum Saints* books by making them available to the public. TPPM only distributes books and DVDs through chaplains. So, if any individuals want to read *Maximum Saints* books or if they want to send *Maximum Saints* books to their incarcerated families, they cannot do it. So, TPPM will make them available so people can purchase the books through book stores and they can send them to their families if they like. All the proceeds from *Maximum Saints* books will be helping TPPM to distribute more free books and DVDs to prisons and homeless shelters.

9. Unexpected Call

I attended Bible college in Korea and in America because I loved theological studies, but I never thought or imagined becoming a minister or a jail chaplain. It was God's plan for me. When He first called me to ministry in

1997, I resisted it. I ran like Jonah and went and bought more than ten rental houses and commercial buildings. Not long after that the housing market fell. I went through lots of financial hardships. I felt I was inside of a fish like Jonah. I suffered and paid the price of running away from my call. It took me about two years to give up my own plans and finally said yes to the call after I wrote a book, *Journey with Jesus*. God told me He had some kind of ministry for me before I responded to the call. So, before I started Iliff School of Theology, I asked Him what He wanted me to do.

The next day the Lord reminded me of my visit to my brother while he was in prison in South Korea. This was the second time I had visited him. My brother ran away from home when my alcoholic father started beating my mother. He was 13 years old when he became homeless. He got involved in gangs, ended up getting in trouble with the law and was incarcerated three times.

When I visited my brother in prison, I was flooded with tears and I just couldn't stop. My brother saw me and said, "Why did you come?" It hurt my brother to see my tears. I couldn't say a word. I walked out of that place in tears. I never went back to see him again. It was too painful for me to see him there. He didn't deserve to be there. If he had a loving and non-violent father, my brother wouldn't have ran away from home.

When God reminded me of the visit, He also reminded me what I wanted to see in my brother's incarceration. I wanted to see only one thing. I was hoping that someone would introduce Jesus to my brother so he could be saved, and find hope and direction in life. That never happened and my brother still is not a Christian.

What I wanted others to do for my brother, is what God was asking me to do. The Lord spoke to me and said, "Go and tell them they are forgiven. Treat them like your brother." I knew then I was called to prison ministry. The Lord blessed me through prison ministry.

If you are a family member of the prisoners, don't just grieve or cry. Find a way to help prisoners and an after care program so you can help others instead of grieving. Pray so that others can help your incarcerated family. Seek God's kingdom first instead of worrying about your family member. He will bless you as you plant the seed of hope with tears. *"He who goes out weeping, carrying seed to sow, will return with songs of joy, carrying sheaves with him."* (Psalm 126:6)

If you are a pastor in a church and want to be a part of the spiritual harvest, save souls and see how the Holy Spirit is blessing people, I encourage you to visit a jail or prison and start a prison ministry in your church. You will receive more than you give. God bless you.

Chapter 5

How to Start Prisoners' Book Project

This chapter is for those who are interested in starting a prisoner's book project similar to *Maximum Saints* books. Some chaplains and volunteers who saw the impact of *Maximum Saints* books asked me how they can start a similar project. Here is the step by step method Transformation Project Prison Ministry (TPPM) took and you can adopt any areas according to your need.

(1) Find a facility where they are open to this project: Ask the inmates to write their stories and edit the stories of other inmates, this encourages the inmates and is good for the facility. Many times inmates have spare time and don't know what to do. If you can convince your chaplain or program department that this will help the inmates and the facility, they will be more open to support this kind of project. Call it a "Writing project for inmates who have experienced transformation."

(2) Find a chaplain or a volunteer who would be committed to gathering stories for this project: You have to work with a person who is committed to gathering stories and then others can help with typing and editing. Find stories that will help others and stories about how God has helped them in their difficult times.

(3) Find a name for this project and create a professional looking brochure: Once people understand your mission and service they will want to donate to your project. You will need to include a section in your brochure with instruction on where to send donations.

(4) You can start a non-profit corporation or find a church

that will support your project. I didn't start with non-profit status right away because of the cost involved. I also wasn't sure how this project would go. In addition, I didn't want to keep track of all the funds, so I decided to find a church. Broomfield United Methodist Church handled the funds and later Park Hill United Methodist church did. Then when I met Laura Nokes-Lang, she started non-profit for TPPM.

(5) Create a consent form: God blessed TPPM with a lawyer who created a consent form to protect TPPM from those who want to use their stories for their own selfish reasons other than helping others or giving God glory by sharing their stories and art work. TPPM does not pay anyone for writing their stories and paying inmates is against the policy of the facility. Also, TPPM does not let inmates use donated material to gain court favor. Anyone can write to their judge for their case but what they donate material is to give God glory and to help others by sharing how God helped them. That is to protect the integrity of our mission. So, find a good lawyer who can help you to create a consent form for your organization.

(6) Make sure your mission is clear: The TPPM mission is to share the love of Jesus Christ through the stories of transformation. I see it two ways: 1) Help people find Christ so they can be saved and find direction in life. 2) To help people grow spiritually so they can help others. Inmates' testimonies are so powerful and God can use them to convert and help others grow in faith. Our focus is clear so it's easy for us to know which story we need to add to the book.

(7) You need to find someone who can convert your typed text into book format: Find a graphic designer for the book cover: Encourage inmates to draw for the book cover.

(8) Find a publisher which will be reasonable. We self publish books and we worked with the following company: RR Donnelley, RR Donnelley & Sons, N9234 Lake Park Road, Appleton, WI 54915 (920) 969-6427. You have to provide all the text and cover in PDF format.

(9) Keep working on fundraising project: TPPM is an interdenominational project. I visited many different churches across denominations. I preached, shared and gave mission presentation to promote this project and people started to donate. The first three years, I was visiting an average of more than 20 churches and organizations every year. Keep knocking on the doors and praying so the Holy Spirit will lead you to where you need to go.

(10) Work with a connection system if you can: Funding is very crucial for this project. I am a United Methodist minister and I feel very fortunate that United Methodist is a connectional system and they approved TPPM project as a mission project. Still, if this project is only supported by United Methodist churches, our mission is limited so that's why I work with many different churches and denominations and organizations.

(11) Contact local media and newspaper companies to see if they want to help you promote your project. Ask them if they want to interview and write an article about your project to promote and raise funds.

Chapter 6

A Prayer of Blessing

"Lord Jesus, bless everyone who reads this book. Let the readers be blessed with your presence and experience healing beyond their imagination, especially the families of the incarcerated and the prisoners all over the world. Bless your people and send the Holy Spirit to raise up your workers inside and outside of prisons, so the revival will sweep over the world. You created us for your glory. Please forgive us of our sin of ignoring you. Lord, anoint this book to save and touch people. Let me proclaim your love and healing power to those who are grief stricken because of their family's incarceration. Please shine your light to those who only see darkness. Help us to be humble before you. Bless us with conviction of sins, and please start it with me. Lord Jesus, help us to look up to you with pure hearts and sincere love for you. Help us to take care of others with your love and compassion especially prisoners and homeless people. Bless prisoners who are reaching out to other prisoners. Wipe the tears and comfort the families of the incarcerated and especially the innocent children. Jesus, bless us with your heart of compassion and love. Free us from selfish, sinful, and violent thoughts, words and behaviors. Wash us with the blood of Jesus Christ, so we can have a clear conscience, that we may know what is right and wrong. I bless you, Lord Jesus, and thank you for helping me to write this book. I give you glory, honor, and praise for what you have done in my life and in my prison ministry, especially with the *Maximum Saints* book project. Holy Spirit, pour out your love and power on those in the world that are hurting and are in need of your healing touch. I love you, Jesus. In Jesus' name I pray. Amen."

Chapter 7

An Invitation

1. An Invitation to Accept Christ:

Do you have an empty heart that cannot be filled with anyone or anything? God can fill your empty heart with His love and forgiveness. Do you feel your life has no meaning, no direction, no purpose, and you don't know where to turn to find the answers? It's time to turn to God. That's the only way you will understand the meaning and the purpose of your life. You will find direction that will lead you to fulfillment and joy. Is your heart broken and hurting, and you don't know how to experience healing? Until we meet Christ in our hearts, we cannot find the peace and healing that God can provide. Jesus can help heal your broken heart. If you don't have a relationship with Christ, this is an opportunity for you to accept Jesus into your heart so you can be saved, find peace and healing from God. Here is a prayer if you are ready to accept Jesus:

"Dear Jesus, I surrender my life and everything to you. I give you all my pain, fear, regret, resentment, anger, worry, and concerns that overwhelm me. I am a sinner. I need your forgiveness. Please come into my heart and my life and forgive all my sins. I believe that you died for my sins and that you have plans for my life. Please heal my broken heart and bless me with your peace and joy. Help me to cleanse my life so I can live a godly life. Help me to understand your plans for my life and help me to obey you. Fill me with the Holy Spirit, and guide me so I can follow your way. I pray this in Jesus' name. Amen."

2. An Invitation for The Transformation Project Prison Ministry (TPPM):

Books and DVDs produced by TPPM are distributed in many jails, prisons, and homeless shelters nationwide free of charge made possible by grants and donations. America has 2.3 million people incarcerated, the largest prison population in the world, and there is a great shortage of inspirational books in many jails and prisons.

"One Million Dream Project"

In 2010, TPPM board decided to expand the ministry goal and started, the "One Million Dream Project." TPPM decided to raise enough funds to distribute one million copies of each book that TPPM has produced for prisoners and homeless people. I ask you to pray for this project so God can help TPPM to reach out to those who cannot speak for themselves, and are in need of spiritual guidance.

TPPM is a 501(c)(3) nonprofit organization, so your donation is 100% tax deductible. If you would like to be a partner in this very important mission of bringing transformation through the message of Christ in prisons and homeless shelters, or want to know more about this project, please visit: www.transformprisons.org.
You can donate on line or you can write a check addressed to:
Transformation Project Prison Ministry
5209 Montview Boulevard
Denver, CO 80207
Phone: 720-951-2629

Website: www.transformprisons.org
Email: transf@gbgmchurches.gbgm-umc.org
Facebook: http://tinyurl.com/yhhcp5g

3. How to purchase *Maximum Saints* books:

This is for individuals who would like to purchase or send a copy to their incarcerated family. TPPM receives lots of requests for individual distribution but we only distribute them through chaplains. All the proceeds from *Maximum Saints* will go to TPPM to distribute more free books and

DVDs to prisons and homeless shelters. To find more about purchasing *Maximum Saints* books, check our website: www.maximumsaints.com. The following books are available, but more books will be available in the future.

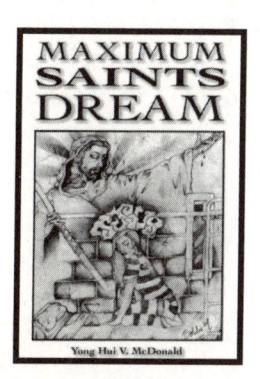

ABOUT THE AUTHOR

Yong Hui V. McDonald, also known as Vescinda McDonald, is a chaplain at Adams County Detention Facility, certified American Correctional Chaplain, spiritual director and on-call hospital chaplain. She founded the Transformation Project Prison Ministry (TPPM) in 2005 and founded GriefPathway Ventures, LLC in 2010 to help others learn how to process grief and healing.

Education:
- Multnomah Bible College, B.A.B.E. (1984)
- Iliff School of Theology, Master of Divinity (2002)
- The Samaritan Counseling & Educational Center, Clinical Pastoral Education (CPE) (2002)
- Rocky Mountain Pastoral Care and Training Center (CPE) (2003)
- Formation Program for Spiritual Directors (2004)

Books and Audio books Written by Yong Hui V. McDonald:
- *Moment by Moment*
- *Journey With Jesus, Visions, Dreams, Meditations & Reflections*
- *Dancing in the Sky, A Story of Hope for Grieving Hearts*
- *Twisted Logic, The Shadow of Suicide*
- *Twisted Logic, The Window of Depression*
- *Dreams & Interpretations, Healing from Nightmares*
- *I Was The Mountain, In Search of Faith & Revival*
- *The Ultimate Parenting Guide, How to Enjoy Peaceful Parenting and Joyful Children*
- *Prisoners Victory Parade, Extraordinary Stories of Maximum Saints & Former Prisoners*
- *Four Voices, How They Affect Our Minds*
- Compiled and published five *Maximum Saints* books under the Transformation Project Prison Ministry.

DVDs produced by Yong Hui:
- *Dancing in The Sky, Mismatched Shoes*
- *Tears of The Dragonfly, Suicide and Suicide Prevention* (CD is also available)

Spanish books produced by Yong Hui:
- *Twisted Logic, The Shadow of Suicide*
- *Journey With Jesus, Visions, Dreams, Meditations & Reflections*

GriefPathway Ventures, LLC, P.O. Box 220, Brighton, CO 80601, Website: www.griefpathway.com
Email: griefpwv@gmail.com